D1404388

MANAGING
WITH THE
POWER OF NLP

> "An excellent toolkit for managers and management developers alike. David has applied a vast range of NLP skills and concepts with the effectiveness and grace that follows from years of first hand experience. Examples, metaphors and diagrams make the book attractive to even the most ardent opponent of jargon and NLP speak."
>
> Kathleen King, Visiting Tutor at London Business School,
> Organizational Development Co-ordinator for the RCN.

> "Finally we have a book written by a master of both NLP and management. This book decodes the jargon of NLP for the manager and shows how this powerful technology can make a manager more effective and productive and a business more profitable. It is a significant contribution to both NLP and business science."
>
> Wyatt Woodsmall, INLPTA, USA.

"Self understanding is a prerequisite for leading and managing others effectively, responsibly and honorably. This essentially practical book gives an insightful, realistic and stimulating way of knowing one's self and others better and of seeing new possibilities, plus help with how to use these insights constructively."

Roy Williams, Chairperson
AMED (Association for Management Education and Development)

MANAGING
WITH THE
POWER OF NLP

neuro-linguistic programing for personal competitive advantage

David Molden

FT Prentice Hall
FINANCIAL TIMES

An imprint of **Pearson Education**

London • New York • Toronto • Sydney • Tokyo • Singapore
Hong Kong • Cape Town • Madrid • Paris • Amsterdam • Munich • Milan

PEARSON EDUCATION LIMITED

Head Office:
Edinburgh Gate
Harlow CM20 2JE
Tel: +44 (0)1279 623623
Fax: +44 (0) 1279 431059
Website: www.pearsoned.co.uk

First published in Great Britain 1996

ISBN 0 273 62063 0

British Library Cataloguing in Publication Data
A CIP catalogue record for this book can be obtained from the British Library.

Typeset by Northern Phototypesetting Co. Ltd, Bolton
Printed and bound in Great Britain by Bell & Bain Ltd, Glasgow

The Publishers' policy is to use paper manufactured from sustainable forests.

David Molden is a director with Quadrant 1 International, a vehicle for helping people be their best in whatever they pursue. David's assignments include 1:1 coaching clients and a range of projects with large corporations, small businesses, and entrepreneurs.

David gained valuable management experience in the IT sector where he learned how to succeed through motivating his teams. He found the experience so personally rewarding that he invested in his own skills and reshaped his career to *be* and *do* what he loves and enjoys most – drawing out the hidden capability from people.

Today he enjoys working as a Peak Performance Mentor with business teams, CEO's and managers across a variety of sectors and in many different countries. He also likes to work with children, building confidence and team skills, and helping them to work with their energy and intuition. He is a Qigong instructor, and author of self-help books published in five languages internationally by Pearson Education. He lives in Oxford, England, with his wife and two sons, and enjoys traveling, writing, music and reading. He has a particular interest in eastern wisdom and philosophy.

contents

section one
SELF AWARENESS

foreword

In the last 25 years or so, the idea of self-development has moved from the far-out fringes of management and people development, to the center stage. Part of this has been due to a shift from "control" to "commitment" strategies in managing organizations. When the dominant model of managing is one of planning, motivating and controlling, those who encounter the notion of people taking charge of their own learning, can see little point in it, dismissing it as being "unbusiness-like" or perhaps "Californian". However, managers and leaders in flat, lean, decentralized structures find it harder to control, and perforce must work through developing commitment – engaging people's hearts and minds, encouraging them to grow to their full capacities and potentials.

This shift has brought into being a wide and proliferating range of methods for self-development. NLP is indeed from California but has travelled well. Coming of age with the Beatles, CND and Catch 22, I have always been wary of "programing" approaches to human development. Because of their strength in creating powerful techniques, they also offer the danger of seeming complete, sufficient, without need of alternative. Yet some of my best friends are trained as engineers, scientists or information specialists, who love their stage models, cognitive maps and social technologies – and they do manage to do some good in the world. As Buddha noted, "It is better to do a little good than to write difficult books."

What comes through in this book is David Molden's openness, friendliness and enthusiasm for learning. NLP with its insights into patterns of thinking, creativity and individual and group "empowerment", has been an influential part of his development. Here you can see some of the results of that learning. It is written very clearly and with clear commitment. It has useful models and engaging activities for improving human communication. It is ecological, anti-authoritarian and for a learning culture in organizations, what more are you looking for?

Mike Pedler
Revans Professorial Fellow at the Revans Centre for
Action Learning and Research, Salford University

Preface

Man, the "paragon of animals," is currently going through an obsession with information technology. The faculty which developed nuclear power, space flight and other technological marvels of our century is now intensely occupied with the silicon chip revolution. The acceleration of scientific discovery in the past 50 years is clearly astounding when you think that it has taken a span of over 2,000 years, from Pythagoras to Isaac Newton, to understand the basic dynamics of our Solar System. One of the reasons for the rapid increase in acceleration could be that today we more readily accept change. Galileo's discovery that the Earth was not at the centre of the universe was suppressed by the Catholic Church because it contradicted their beliefs. The Church would not accept Galileo's different view.

The human mind has the faculty for innovation and stagnation; for creation and destruction; for joy and sadness. The human mind is also the most powerful computer on Earth, and at this period in history it is wrapped up with the information technology explosion. Ever since Charles Babbage built the first computing machine in the 19th century our obsession with computers has led to many innovations in scientific and business applications. Many of the developments made possible by the computer are quite ingenious, yet I wonder just how different things might be if the primary focus for change and innovation were to shift from things to people; from outward observation to inward reflection; from the silicon chip to the human mind.

Imagine a commercial organization which values the development of the human mind as a methodology for progress. Its mission statement might be "to develop minds and to innovate, creating a healthy, stimulating and nurturing business community for the benefit of everyone." Then imagine a business environment where processes and problems are clearly separated from personalities. Our organizations are moving in the right direction with improvement programs like *TQM*, *Re-engineering* and *Best Practice*, all of which are based on

What a piece of work is man! How noble in reason! How infinite in faculty! in form and moving, how express and admirable! in action how like an angel! in apprehension, how like a god! the beauty of the world! the paragon of animals!

Hamlet, Hamlet,
WILLIAM SHAKESPEARE

[1] Pedler, Burgoyne and Boydell, *The Learning Company: A Strategy for Sustainable Development*, McGraw Hill (1991).

the concept of learning. Currently, *The Learning Organization*[1] is out front leading the field and lighting the way for forward-thinking management teams.

Some time in the future we will invest more time in learning how to use our brain. We will learn to communicate wisely and to adapt our thinking in ways we have yet to discover. The future potential of our world relies upon the development of the human mind, and the technology to begin tapping this potential is with us right now.

■ Neuro . . . what?!!!

[2] Bandler and Grinder, *Frogs into Princes*, Real People Press, (1979).

In 1976 Richard Bandler and John Grinder[2] sat together in a cabin in the hills above Santa Cruz, California, and thought of a name for their groundbreaking research into human communication. The term they arrived at was Neuro-linguistic Programing, or NLP for short, a most apt and descriptive name yet one that continues to confuse many people and which, unfortunately, may prevent them from exploring NLP further. Perhaps the concepts and jargon of NLP seem so different to some people that they would rather remain with conventional theory. As Galileo discovered, this type of thinking is restrictive to human development, innovation and progress in general.

Maybe your decision to read this book means that you are motivated to seek new perspectives on learning, communication and personal development. Perhaps you are curious to explore the differences found in management thinking and behavior. Perspective and difference in thinking are at the root of all behavior: consider the differences in thinking of Adolf Hitler and Mahatma Gandhi and the subsequent diversity of behavior. How we use our mind determines our results.

Whatever your motivation for picking up the book, if, like an increasing number of business managers you want to develop effective communication skills; if you want to accomplish greater things with perceived ease and excellence – or simply if you want to improve all your results, stay with me for the rest of the journey to discover the power of NLP – a science of perspective and difference.

David Molden

key to margin symbols

In the margin you will find various pieces of information.

NLP This signifies one of a number of NLP principles around which NLP is built, and you will find them invaluable in helping you to organize your thinking for maximum effect.

This indicates an emphasis of the main learning points, and is included to support your retention of the material.

This indicates where you will find an exercise in the main body of the text.

acknowledgments

Firstly, to the two pioneers and originators of NLP – Richard Bandler and John Grinder, and to the many people responsible for the wide variety of developments and applications. To my teachers Brad Waldron, Willie Monteiro, Wyatt Woodsmall, Marvin Oka, Richard Diehl, Dave Marshall, Robert Smith, and to all my students for investing their time in my personal development. To Robert Dilts for his work on neurological levels, his insights to belief structures and his modeling of Walt Disney and Albert Einstein. To every other contributor to the field of NLP, too many to mention by name, and to Patrick E. Merlevede for his Internet web-page of NLP and company listings.

A very special thank you to Brad Waldron, Mike O'Sullivan and Ray Perkins for providing their own unique perspectives on my ideas and material. To Jim Froud for sharing his curiosity and observations of Oxford folk, and especially to Julia, Ross and Charlie for living with and giving encouragement to an almost eccentric hologram for the past four months.

introduction

If you are inspired to look beyond conventional teaching models for *new* ways of developing management competence, this book is written for you. It is different from many conventional management books in that it concentrates on *you*, the manager, and how *you* can change to develop greater degrees of excellence rather than how you can change others. *You are the role model for your people. You are the example of how to be in the organization*. If you are motivated to learn and develop yourself, NLP will help you discover how to use or *program* your neurology and language to get the results you really want for yourself, your team and your organization. I will explain and give practical examples of how NLP can be used by all managers from the *fresh new youngbloods* to the *not so fresh but seasoned managers*, and *top corporate strategists*. I will share with you my personal experiences of using NLP as a management learning technology, and experiences of others in business from whom I have learned. I will also be inviting you to work through some exercises so that you can begin to practice NLP and experience results for yourself.

This is a personal development book for managers. While writing it, my intention has been to concentrate on the practical management applications of NLP, adding just enough supporting theory and jargon for you to understand how it works. As a developer, I have put NLP to work both in and out of the classroom, and so throughout the book I will be sharing with you applications from my own experience as a manager, and from my management training courses. First I will set the backdrop for chapter 1 by sharing with you an early personal experience of managing *without* the power of NLP.

What is managing?

I remember being given my first real management challenge – setting up a regional service operation from scratch. The task came with full membership of the fraternity known as *management*. The times were

Neuro –
what we do with our brains.

Linguistic –
verbal and non-verbal language we use to organize and communicate our thoughts.

Programing –
the unique way each individual puts it all together to produce behavior.

NLP is a learning technology

exciting at Computacenter, working in the young but fast-growing microcomputer industry, and I desperately wanted to succeed and make my mark on the management ladder.

The first couple of weeks was a period of orientation to my new environment, and then on Monday morning of the third week I was suddenly struck by the stark reality of my situation. What were my objectives? What was expected of me? What responsibility and authority did I have? I had been so full of excitement at the interview with my manager that these questions hadn't occurred to me at that time. The promotion gave me such an overwhelming feeling of achievement that I had blocked out any rational questions concerning the role I had been given. It very soon became apparent, however, that whatever plans there may have been for the business in that region making a success of it was all down to me!

My personal experience of being induced into management is not untypical, so I later discovered, from the experience of many of my colleagues and peers in other companies. I never found the "how to" guide of managing, and so my skills gradually evolved with experience. From my role models I learned how to mismanage extremely well – thankfully I decided not to follow their examples. If you're a young manager early into your career perhaps you can relate to my story. If you are more my age, seasoned with experience gained over a number of years, it is likely that the challenges before you will stem from the changing organizational environment where downsizing, de-layering, restructuring and re-engineering are recognized as basic ingredients for the future health and fitness of business.

Some organizations are so focussed on health, fitness and efficiency that whole departments and management teams are being made redundant and forced to re-apply for a fewer number of jobs. The unsuccessful remain unemployed. Assessment centres analyze personality, skills and decision making abilities to ensure that only the most intelligent, articulate and multi-faceted individuals are selected for employment. For their reward, these fortunate people get to work in a climate that is becoming increasingly more complex and where solutions to problems require greater degrees of creativity and sophistication.

Tom Peters[1] in his book *Thriving on Chaos* suggests that tomorrow's winners will be those that are capable of dealing proactively

[1] Tom Peters, *Thriving on Chaos – Handbook for a Management Revolution*, Pan Books, (1987).

with the chaos that is the result of increasing competitiveness. So if chaos is something we can thrive upon, the crucial question is: what skills does a manager need to get results in this chaotic environment?

Conventional methods of learning are not coping with the demands from managers in today's environment. Convention doesn't have the speed, flexibility and generative qualities needed for personal development amid the accelerating pace of the modern business world. The challenge for today's generation of managers is in developing the ability to learn at a superfast pace and in generating personal strategies to dissect and resolve ambiguity. The challenge for the seasoned manager is in maintaining the personal resources needed to stimulate personal and group innovation – a vital requirement for survival in a world that seems to fall further into chaos and disorder. Top executives, MDs and CEOs will need a technology for designing innovative corporate strategies, with the flexibility to adapt in response to market forces and stay ahead of the field.

An inappropriate corporate strategy can have a devastating effect on the organization, its employees and its customers for a long time. The growing number of consultancies offering executive counseling services is indicative of the increasing uncertainty and nervousness of many business strategists as a result of intense competition and high levels of complexity. So, the answer to the question "what is managing?" is simple. Managing is creating order out of chaos. Regardless of your experience, status, intellect, role or objectives, NLP provides the learning to develop potential and realize success – while creating order from chaos. And the challenge here is in creating an order that is capable of changing and evolving in sympathy with the needs of people and the business.

Managing is not so much about *what* to do, rather *how* to do. To be effective as a manager in today's fast-changing world of business requires effective learning strategies. Strategies are *how* you achieve your desired objectives, and NLP is one of the most effective *how to* technologies that exist in the area of human communication, learning and change. You will discover precisely how, through an increasing self awareness, you can develop a generative learning ability in three core role dimensions – leadership, communication, and innovation. Increased self awareness leads to more control over your thinking and behavior. This generates the flexibility needed to build effective strategies – for any management challenge.

Working environments are becoming more complex with increasing diversity and ambiguity.

Managers need the capability to generate ever more creative and sophisticated business solutions.

Managing is creating order out of chaos.

Increased self awareness leads to more control over your thinking and behavior.

Feedback

It is worth exploring the idea of feedback since many people believe that learning from feedback is an unconscious process, that is they don't have to spend time thinking about feedback because learning happens as a natural and automatic process. And they are absolutely right. However, the learning which happens automatically is not necessarily the learning you want. Managers who continually fire-fight use feedback in this way. They use feedback to maintain their system of fire-fighting taking them from one crisis to another. I have known some brilliant fire-fighters in my time, and it is their automatic responses to feedback which keep them operating in well developed grooves. Unfortunately, the only learning they experience helps them to put out more fires in different ways – with no prevention scheme in sight!

Learning which happens automatically is not necessarily the learning you want.

This is one way of dealing with feedback. Another way is to think that feedback is a personal attack, become defensive and reject the feedback as someone else's failure. The most useful feedback is free of judgment about its nature, intention, emotion or any other type of contamination. Treat it as a scientist would a laboratory experiment – describing precisely what you see and what you hear. To say "he didn't like my proposal – he can't appreciate the quality of what we are presenting to him" is to contaminate vital feedback with likes/dislikes and judgments about what can/can't be appreciated. It is better to accept the feedback, discover why the proposal wasn't accepted and do something positive about it.

The most useful feedback is free of judgment.

Choice

We all make many choices throughout the course of a day. How we choose and what we choose narrows down our options. At an airport I can choose from a number of destinations. If I choose New York, and mid-flight I hear a report of bad weather there, it's too bad – I'm on the plane to New York. Behavioral choice is much like this, and the consequences of choosing inappropriately must be accepted and lived with.

There is also a choice over how you exercise choice. Have you ever got on the wrong bus or driven to the wrong destination out of habit?

This often happens when you make the same journey regularly, but for once you need to go somewhere different. Because you are pre-occupied thinking about something else, you choose the wrong bus or freeway exit. You can allow your habits to make automatic choices for you, or you can put some higher quality conscious thought behind them. Sometimes in business, seemingly small choices about what you say at an interview or a negotiation can have major consequences on you, the business and its employees.

Generative development

The book is constructed around an all embracing "generative management development" model. The concept behind the model is simple. You become self-aware by accepting uncontaminated feedback which you process within three core management dimensions – leadership, communication, and innovation (refer to figure 1).

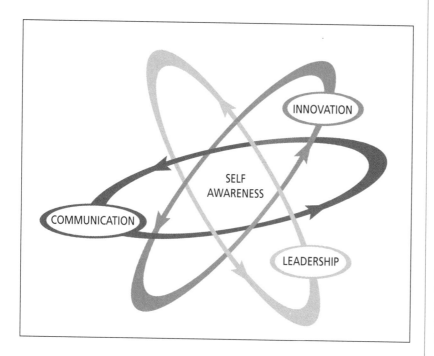

■ FIGURE 1
Generative
management
development
model

Managers who invest little time in self-analysis rarely change what they do and what they say . . .

. . . their results often reflect this behavioral consistency and inflexibility.

You operate in the organization as a leader, communicator, and innovator. You get feedback from your efforts in each of these three dimensions which you can either ignore or learn from. If you want to improve your operational effectiveness you will choose to analyze your feedback so that you can make necessary changes to your behavior. Personal effectiveness is improved by investing time in thinking about how to change what you do and what you say (behavior).

Managers who invest little time in this activity (you probably know some in your organization) rarely change what they do and say – and their results often reflect this behavioral consistency and inflexibility.

So spending time analyzing your feedback and making intelligent choices in the three dimensions of leadership, communication, and innovation will improve self awareness and enhance personal development. In this way the model is generative, which means that you are constantly generating your own learning and development in all *four* key dimensions:

Self awareness
How well you know yourself; what makes you tick; creating direction and setting outcomes for yourself; being a role model and improving your capability to integrate new learning.

Leadership
How you organize yourself and the methods you use to motivate, direct, develop and get the most from your team.

Communication
How you connect with yourself and with others.

Innovation
How you provide variety, create new ideas and foster an environment of learning and innovation.

You operate, get feedback, and change behavior according to the results you want. In each section of the book you will be introduced to various NLP techniques that will help you to increase the quality and quantity of uncontaminated feedback, develop generative thought processes and increase your operational flexibility in each of these four dimensions.

Getting the most from this book

Can you remember the first time you tried to ride a bicycle? How awkward it seemed to be attempting to balance on two thin wheels while moving your feet in a circular motion. Being aware of how your feet needed to be connecting with the pedals and getting the right balance to steer the bike in the right direction both at the same time wasn't easy, was it? Then you tried it a second time, and then a third until eventually, after many bruised knees, you finally mastered the metal beast and began to innovate with new ways of being on a bike – ever done no hands?

This is a good example of how we learn. The first time you try something completely new you can feel awkward doing the new thing. To make any progress you have to overcome this initial barrier to learning and practice by making adjustments in accordance with the feedback you are getting. Eventually you lose the awkwardness and become comfortable doing the new thing. With further practice and more feedback you get to the stage where you can ride your bike with ease and grace without thinking consciously about it. This is the approach you need for the practical exercises in this book which will present you with many new ways of thinking and being. Practice and you will reap the benefits.

Throughout the book you will be presented with opportunities to practice NLP techniques. If some appear odd or peculiar to you, that is a sign of approaching something new – outside of your existing knowledge of learning. Stay with the material, explore it and remain curious to discover more. As you continue through the book you may notice that your own perception of learning is changing and that generating a greater self awareness is becoming even more natural to you.

Chaos often breeds life, when order breeds habit.
HENRY B ADAMS
(1838–1918)
American historian

SELF AWARENESS

ULTIMATE FLEXIBILITY

- ■ **The autopilot – your unconscious mind**

- ■ **What is flexibility?**

- ■ **Removing limitations to developing flexibility**
Identity – *Who?* / Values and beliefs – *Why?* / Capability – *How?*/
Behavior – *What?* /Environment – *Where? When?*

The chains of habit are too weak to be felt until they are too strong to be broken.
DR SAMUEL JOHNSON
(1709–84) British poet

Your unconscious mind is an auto-pilot for your body functions and your habits while your conscious mind controls the parts of your neurology needed to read and interpret the words you are looking at right now.

We are very adept at repeating a process once we have learned how to do it.

The auto-pilot – your unconscious mind

One human trait that distinguishes people from other species on this planet is the ability to self-analyze. We are able to step out of, or disconnect from, our present situation and generate thoughts about past, current, future, and imaginary events. This is often referred to as being "preoccupied", where your focus of attention becomes directed inward. How many times, while traveling home from work, have you caught yourself running a movie in your mind of some incident earlier in the day – and upon arriving home you're unable to recall the journey?

This review activity is carried out by the conscious part of your mind while it is disconnected from the external world around you, and your unconscious mind takes over processing the input signals from your five senses. If you have never driven a car, can you imagine working all the controls without thinking about it *and* driving safely? If you are a relatively new driver you may not yet have developed your co-ordination of the car's controls to the extent that driving safely requires little of your conscious attention. This will develop over time. If you are an experienced driver, you will know what it is like to have arrived at your destination not remembering anything about driving there.

This latter example is an excellent demonstration of the unconscious mind being on auto-pilot and taking over control of habitual behaviors while your conscious mind carries out some inner processing.

From this example we can extract three learning points. The first one is that we are very adept at repeating a process once we have learned how to do it. This is how habits are formed and maintained (fire-fighting managers are particularly skilled in this area). The second point is that once we have learned a new habit it can be difficult to break out of, especially as we have to consciously think about the habit in order to avoid doing it. Have you ever tried driving an automatic car for the first time and found yourself fumbling for the clutch and gearstick? This is one reason why people find it so hard to quit smoking, stick to a diet or change the way they relate to people at work.

The third point is that change very often requires "unlearning" some unwanted habitual behaviors before learning more useful ones. Car drivers become dangerous through the habits they develop – like driving too close to the car in front. Learning to become a safe driver starts with unlearning these dangerous habits before moving on to learn new ones like advanced anticipation skills. In this section on self-analysis you will learn precisely *how* you communicate with yourself, and *how* you program your autopilot to intentionally and consciously learn new habits. This chapter contains a model of learning and change that you will want to return to many times as you progress through the book, but first of all, let's take a look at some issues around flexibility using a metaphor to represent a common organizational challenge with a range of typical responses.

Thinking in negatives – what can't be done or what isn't possible acts on the unconscious as a limiting and disempowering influence.

Take the "t" out of can't! Instead, think what can be done and what is possible.

What is flexibility?

Here's a question for you to contemplate: *Can you fit a square peg into a round hole?* What kind of answers would you expect to get?

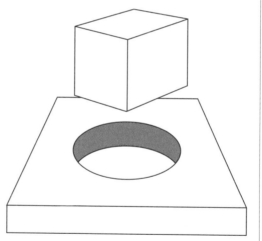

1 No – I can't do it.
This is a *defeat* type of response. It reacts to the situation and information as presented, and concludes with defeat from the ultimate limitation to flexibility – the word *can't*. It is a disempowering word that communicates a message of inflexibility and self-doubt to your unconscious mind and which programs you to focus on the impossible rather than the possible. The word is also untrue in many contexts where it is used. How do you know it can't be done?

A more truthful response would be *I haven't found a way of doing it yet*. In a commercial environment, customers are not interested in what you *can't* do for them – they want to know what you *can* do.

Language is a powerful influence on our behavior and learning ability and I will explain exactly how it works in chapter 2.

2 *Give me a big enough mallet and I'll try.* This is a *reaction* type of response. It is an improvement on the first, but only slightly. It demonstrates determination but directs all energy into one reactive solution. There is a great danger that the peg, hole, and mallet will all become damaged in the process.

3 *Yes if I reshape the square peg so that it fits.* This is a *sophistry* type of response. In order for the peg to fit I must learn how to reshape square pegs so that they fit round holes. I never cease to be amazed at the amount of effort, resource and sophistication companies invest in reshaping different systems and structures that are either inappropriate or unworkable. This third response is little improvement over the second, and it is certainly no more flexible. It still reacts to the situation and information as presented.

4 *What would be the purpose for the fit and how did a square peg ever come to be offered to a round hole in the first place?* This is a *curiosity* type of response, and the most flexible for a number of reasons. Its curiosity seeks to identify the intention behind the question, looking for more information outside of the frame presented. The result is a clearer picture of the situation with which to aid a decision-making process. This response challenges the question, i.e. it does not presuppose that the objective is to fit a square peg into a round hole.

Some years ago, a friend of mine working for a competitor organization, was approached by a director with a plan for developing a central IT support facility to cover the UK. My friend was delighted at having been given this strategically important project to manage and he accepted all the presuppositions that came with it, including this one – *that UK analysts wanted a centralized support facility.*

Three years later the support facility was in a totally confused mess. It had a reputation for poor service, the management team were disunited over the basic purpose and direction for the department, and it was losing money. The UK analysts who were the clients of the service had not been consulted, and they could see no benefit in the investment. They wanted local support groups. This situation could possibly have been avoided if the presuppositions contained in the original brief had been challenged. The support group was eventually broken up and dissolved.

Being flexible means having an attitude of mind that produces desired results regardless of the present situation, its complexities, its ambiguities, its pace, its expectations, its culture, its presuppositions, and its political environment. In systems theory[1] – which has much in common with NLP's holistic approach to learning and change – there is a principle called the law of requisite variety which states that "in order to successfully adapt and survive, a member of a system needs a certain amount of flexibility, and that flexibility has to be proportional to the potential variation or the uncertainty in the rest of the system." In the context of management this means that managers must never be content with one solution, rather they must challenge presuppositions, look at influences in the wider system of the organization, and generate as many alternative courses of action to cover all possible eventualities.

Whenever you are faced with a challenge, you will have four basic choices of response:

1 Defeat;
2 Reaction;
3 Sophistry;
4 Curiosity.

The flexible manager will choose option 4.

Removing limitations to developing flexibility

One NLP principle is that you have all the resources you need to succeed. The problem for many people is that they create limitations for themselves. You have already learned how habits of thinking and language can create limitations, and you will be introduced to many other causes through the chapters of this book. At this point I want

Challenging presuppositions helps to make sense of seemingly ambiguous situations.

[1] Ashby W Ross, *Introduction to cybernetics*, Chapman & Hall Ltd, London, 1956

NLP

"In order to successfully adapt and survive, a member of a system needs a certain amount of flexibility, and that flexibility has to be proportional to the potential variation or the uncertainty in the rest of the system."

NLP

You have all the resources you need to succeed.

[2] Bateson G, *Steps to an ecology of mind*, Ballantine Books, NY, 1972.

to explore five levels of learning, communication and change[2] that are key to developing ultimate flexibility of thinking and behavior. The five levels are:

1 Identity;
2 Values and beliefs;
3 Capabilities;
4 Behavior;
5 Environment.

Figure 1.1 shows these levels within a contextual frame as each level can change across contexts. These levels will be referred to many times throughout the book.

■ **FIGURE 1.1**
Levels of learning, communication and change

CONTEXT

1 Identity

how you think of yourself shapes your . . .

2 Values and beliefs

what is important to you,

and what you believe in influences your . . .

3 Capabilities

your knowledge and skills direct your . . .

4 Behavior

what you do and say determines your RESULTS in the . . .

5 Environment

in which you choose to operate

CONTEXT

■ Identity – *who?*

If you never do anything different again in your whole life, your identity will remain the same. Some people live their lives in this way. People who make career moves, and become successful in their new careers, start by unconsciously reframing their identity. They often don't think of it in this way at all – people rarely wake up in the morning and say "I've decided to change my identity," but that's what actually happens at an unconscious level. Take a few moments to think about your professional identity and complete this statement: "I am . . .?" The words you use to describe yourself are labels for your identity.

Some companies go mad with labels – *the deputy to the deputy to the CEO's chief administrator*. Others have settled for a system of grading – *manager grade 2*. There are far too many names and labels for employees in organizations. Labels put meaning to things and so by their very nature influence how we think about them (I am currently looking for a label to replace *subordinate* which, sadly, is still used in organizations and in many conventional management courses). The label *manager* implies *coping*. The label *leader* implies *one whose example is followed*.

These meanings contradict one another. No wonder there is so much ambiguity and disparity in the way people are treated in some organizations. A more apt word for today's business societies, and one which encompasses the roles of both *manager* and *leader* is "developer." You may find alternative words more acceptable to your own particular organizational roles.

When I first began to train people my title was "Training Manager" and I thought of myself as a manager first and a trainer second. This is natural as I had been managing for a long time and training was a completely new concept to me. This thinking caused me to *manage* my delegates instead of *training* them – I was more concerned about the course schedule, timing and logistics than my delegates' learning. My thinking has greatly matured since then, and I must thank my early students for helping me to cross the threshold from manager to developer.

I now have five different professional roles which could be conventionally labeled as: manager, trainer, consultant, writer and learner. I find these labels very restricting which is why I call myself a *developer* – a label that puts a meaning to each of my roles. As a writer I produce development materials rather than books. As a manager I contribute to a team by developing the direction for some and providing development for all. As a consultant I offer clients alternative development options. I run learning workshops rather than

The words you use to describe and think about your roles can greatly influence what you do to fulfill each role.

training courses. I am a developer, and I reinforce this identity by using the labels that fit my perception of what a developer is. Identity labels greatly influence your auto-pilot and it is here, at the level of identity, that you are able to start making the most significant and impactful changes to your performance.

 **EXERCISE 1**

Identity

Here's an exercise that presupposes your ability to become even more flexible than you are now. The objective is for you to think of the labels you currently apply to your professional roles and consider whether there may be more appropriate labels that will help you to be ultimately more flexible and successful in those roles.

On the left hand side of table 1 write one label per line for each of your professional roles. Then for each label in turn, run a movie in your mind of a specific time when you were performing this role. It's OK to just let yourself become fully connected with a situation that you want to improve because you know that you have the ability to switch off the movie at any time – you are in control here . . . so make the movie vivid by fully concentrating on it . . . make it a bright, colorful, moving 3D picture . . . add surround-sound so that you can hear the words of the conversations you are having . . . and when you are fully connected with the experience, . . . notice what you say and do, and if you notice parts of your movie that cause you to feel uncomfortable, ask yourself: *what's going on here?* And then ask yourself these questions: *how could I have been even more flexible in my approach to this situation? What could I change in order to improve my results here?*

For example, imagine you are the manager in charge of a helpdesk and you identify one of your role labels as an "information organizer." As you connect with a typical day, you may focus on collecting and filing information logged from your customers using time that could perhaps be better utilized to reduce the customer's dependency on your service. A more useful role label might be "educator." This exercise will generate some different labels for each of your roles. Write these labels on the right hand side of table 1 opposite the conventional role labels. Have a go at this exercise now. If it makes you think about how you perceive your roles – that is a good sign.

	Conventional role labels	More useful role labels
1		
2		
3		
4		
5		
6		
7		

■ TABLE 1
Identity labels

Identity metaphors
are very effective
ways of adding
meaning to your
roles.

How did you get on? Did you generate some labels that are perhaps more useful than the conventional labels? Have you widened the scope of your professional identity? What you have just done is to generate some identity labels that perhaps suggest different or alternative behavioral choices for *what* you could do to be more flexible around your identity. Later in the book you will be going through some exercises to give you the *how* of increasing behavioral flexibility. Some labels you may have come up with are: *questioner, analyst, innovator, compass (giving direction to others), developer, researcher, information gatherer, shepherd, nurse, grandfather, disseminator.* These are just a few ideas, some of which are more metaphorical than others. Identity metaphors are very effective ways of adding meaning to your roles.

I once knew a manager who thought of herself as a *lion tamer* because that is how she felt about her main role of sales training manager in an aggressively competitive organization. Her delegates needed to unlearn many negative behaviors that were irrelevant in a new marketplace. It was only after they realized the consequences of their usual approach to customers that they could begin to learn new consultative selling techniques – they had to be *tamed* first.

One service manager was so focussed on procedures that she alienated and demotivated all her staff by constantly monitoring their time-keeping to the minute! She identified very strongly with procedures but had little identity as a people developer, enabler and strategist. All her key people eventually left to join other parts of the organization.

A support centre manager identified with administration to such an extent that he hadn't recognized the importance of providing direction for his supervisors. Needless to say the results were quite catastrophic for the whole department because the manager hadn't identified with a director role.

You can create any identity you wish for yourself as a first means towards achieving the type of results usually accredited to the chosen identity, but there are two health warnings that go with this:

1 A poor man one day decided to become a millionaire and every day from then on he put all his energy into making money. One day he succeeded but in the process his wife left him and his children became drug

addicts. Make sure your new identities are in harmony with your human environment which includes you and the people in your life.

2 Deciding upon new identities is only a start. Progress is likely to be limited unless values and beliefs are adopted to nurture the new identity, and new skills acquired so that you have the capability to perform. Identity changes can get you to think and act differently – getting results with new behaviors requires capability.

■ Values and beliefs – *why?*

Values and beliefs determine *why* you do anything. They determine purpose and support or limit your capabilities. Values are things that are important to you, and there are two types of values – means values and end values. It is important for me to exercise regularly (means value) because I value my health (end value). Your end values in a professional context will be the reasons why you do what you do – the satisfaction intrinsic to the job. If you are not getting any job satisfaction then you will not be feeding your values and you are likely to be suffering from stress. Means values feed end values, and they are very powerful – providing you with the motivation to get things done. For example:

- I enjoy fussing with small details in student materials for my courses because (this means) *quality* will be assured.
- I demand high *quality* from myself and my team because (by this means) our department will have a *professional image*.
- It's important to maintain a *professional image* because (by this means) we will get higher and more prestigious responsibilities to *challenge* us.
- Being provided with greater *challenges* (means that) *development* opportunities will be created for me and my team.

> END VALUE = development

Ricardo Semler,[3] owner of Semco S/A, a Brazilian manufacturing company, introduced radical new business processes, reduced hierarchy to three levels and began to trust employees to take the right decisions without having to check with management. In conven-

Values are things that are important to you.

Means values feed end values, and they are very powerful. They provide you with the motivation to get things done.

[3] Semler R, *Maverick*, Warner Books.

Beliefs support and reinforce our values – they are like the glue that holds them together. Our beliefs have little to do with any reality other than our own.

tional terms the company has little control and virtually no discipline. During the period of change some middle managers left the company because they could no longer identify with the new roles they were being asked to perform. After all, they had originally been employed as decision-makers, problem solvers and people managers, and these roles were no longer reserved for "managers" by the new order in Semoco.

Values also change as our life situations change. If we suddenly need more money to maintain a standard of living then this might become a higher level value. If our relationships with loved ones become difficult we may begin to divert our attention and energy to re-establishing harmony in the family. In most cases, job-related values will decrease in importance when there are major deficits at the more basic levels of human need such as remuneration and belonging. Beliefs support and reinforce our values – they are like the glue that holds them together. Our beliefs have little to do with any reality other than our own, and our senses are extremely efficient at filtering out information that might contradict a belief, and at discovering information that might support a belief.

Beliefs are more opinions than fact. Here's a popular scenario to demonstrate the power of belief:

> *Do you believe that there is life on other planets with the technology to visit Earth?*

NLP

Whatever you believe, it's true for you.

There are believers and disbelievers in this theory. The interesting thing to notice is that if you were to gather a dozen from each camp on a hilltop to witness a reported UFO sighting, the disbelievers would come up with all kinds of descriptions that support the UFO being an Earth construction or some illusion, while the believers would be more willing to explore the possibility of it really being an UFO. The beliefs held by each group influence their information processing in different ways and will support their values in some way. NLP provides the principle that: whatever you believe, it's true for you.

An amusing story which emphasizes the power of beliefs extremely well can be found in Robert Dilts's book *Changing belief systems with NLP*[4] which tells of a psychiatric patient who believed he was a corpse. He wouldn't eat or drink anything. For some time the psychiatrist attempts to convince him that he is alive. One day the psychiatrist asked "do corpses bleed?" – "Of course they don't," replied the patient after which the psychiatrist pricked the patient's finger and drew blood. Upon noticing the blood dripping from his finger the patient commented "I'll be damned. Corpses *do* bleed!"

As a developer, one of the more frequent requests I get from my customers is to develop confidence, and this has now become a common feature in many of my personal development courses. The critical elements involved in developing confidence are *belief* and *identity*. Let me refer to one example of this in the area of managing meetings.

> *Being suddenly faced with chairing or facilitating a meeting with senior directors and/or a group of senior specialists, a limiting belief about your capability to communicate with these people is likely to constrain your performance and therefore your results. If the limiting belief is strong enough, those present at the meeting are likely to pick up low-confidence signals from your body language and voice tonality. This, in turn, could influence how they communicate with you. Your limiting belief would also render any knowledge or skill about chairing meetings relatively ineffective in this case.*

Beliefs can change with experience. If you do well at this meeting the experience will help to whittle away at any limiting belief you may have about your ability to communicate effectively with these groups. Unfortunately, for many people, this experience takes a long time to gather, and some people never realize their true potential at all. Limiting beliefs create unresourceful states of mind and body. If you are lacking confidence you are not in the best "state" to deal with the situation. Unresourceful states require energy to sustain them – energy that should be applied to the external problem, not the internal dilemma happening in your neurology!

Confidence plays an important part in the acquisition of skills, and it can begin to develop through the use of appropriate identity labels

[4] Dilts R, *Changing belief systems with NLP*, Meta Publications, 1990.

The critical elements involved in developing confidence are *belief* and *identity*.

Unresourceful states require energy to sustain them – energy that should be applied to the external problem, not the internal dilemma happening in your neurology!

and beliefs. This is the science of learning. When these components of your neurology are aligned you are in a more resourceful state to learn and develop new capabilities.

I spent some time in a workshop with a friend who works as an independent consultant. The purpose of the workshop was to explore the dynamics of a number of components of personality and to analyze how they were constructed. My friend built the following profile of himself:

Identity
A combination of Mother Theresa and Christopher Columbus (a helper of great integrity and a desire for leading others to new pathways of learning and adventure).

End values
- *To be recognized as a mentor to other people*
- *To be at the leading edge of personal development*
- *To improve my own capabilities*
- *To sustain a certain quality of life for my family*

Means values
- *To analyze and understand others' problems*
- *To understand more about myself*
- *To be highly active in many networks*
- *To make lots of new friends*
- *To be honest and ecological with myself and others*
- *To discover new development techniques and ideas*
- *To maintain a respectable level of income*

Beliefs
- *Everyone needs a mentor*
- *Mentors must invest time developing themselves*
- *Removing limitations is easy*
- *People like me because I listen to them*
- *There are parts of my neurology that I don't yet understand*
- *All progress is made through learning and personal development*

This friend of mine is a very capable and successful personal development consultant. People praise his capabilities, compassion, understanding and companionship. His business is successful. His identity, values and beliefs all complement one another, and his behavior is totally congruent with all levels of his neurology. If you wanted to become a successful personal development consultant I would highly recommend modeling these attributes of identity, values and beliefs.

Throughout the book you will have the opportunity to practice accessing resourceful states for various situations, and trying out different values and beliefs to support and develop your identity. You may also wish to modify identity labels as you progress through the book. You will also be introduced to some excellent techniques for making change, at all levels, happen quickly.

Values and beliefs

 EXERCISE 2

Here's an exercise to get you thinking about your own values and beliefs. It is more useful to put down your answers as they occur than to concern yourself with whether a value is end or means, or whether a response is a value or belief.

Answer each question in turn. The purpose of question 1 is to elicit a means value. The purpose of question 2 is to elicit higher level values that could be means or end values. If you run out of responses to this question you have probably reached an end value. Think of at least three different answers for question 2. The purpose of question 3 is to elicit the beliefs that support your values. Think of at least four beliefs that support each set of values. If you're not sure whether something is a belief, a means value or end value, that's OK – just put down your thoughts anyway.

Get a first draft down as quickly as you can, then review what you have written and consider the potency of each value and each belief.

Q1 *What is it you value about your job that if it were taken away your job satisfaction would decrease significantly?*

A _____

Q2 *And what does this value get for you?*

A _____

A _____

A _____

Q3 *What must you believe in order to value the items above?*

A _____

A _____

A _____

A _____

A _____

How did you get on with this exercise? This may be the first time you have ever questioned your reasons and purposes for doing what you do. My intention at this stage is to present you with a basic knowledge of how you can develop behavioral flexibility. As a developer, I believe it is unethical to forcibly change people or manipulate them in any way. Change will only occur when you want the change for yourself.

If, during this and subsequent chapters you decide to adopt different or additional identities, values and beliefs, you will find the techniques offered to you to be very effective. You may be content to reshape square pegs, or to wield heavy mallets. However, I do encourage you to continually question the potency and usefulness of your values and beliefs. Are they enabling you to become the most flexible component of your organizational system?

■ Capability – *how?*

Capability can be defined as *how you apply knowledge and generate behavior to achieve a goal*. In most organizations you will find that the term most commonly used to talk about capability and behavior is "skill." However, in order to understand how a skill is developed it is more useful to work with capabilities.

For example, let's consider a manager who has been asked to lead an important negotiation. I shall assume he has a specific goal which he wants to achieve. Over time he will have learned a large number of words that make up his vocabulary, and he may have learned a specific structure or format for negotiating either from a company procedure document, a book, a film or from a training course. This is knowledge. The capability is in *how* the knowledge is put to use,

It is unethical to forcibly change people or manipulate them in any way.

and this *how* is dependent upon the distinctions he makes around the meeting activity.

These distinctions will generate his behavior – what he says and does in response to each interaction. Does he continue listening and watching, or begin talking? Which words does he choose when it's his turn to speak? Who should he address? What should his body language be saying?

Capability is also influenced by all the levels of learning above it – identity, values and beliefs. If the manager in our example does not identify with the role of negotiator, his negotiating capability will be to a low standard. His values and beliefs may influence the goal he sets for himself. He may believe the negotiation is a lost cause, or that it will be tough. His expectations and goals will be set in response to his beliefs which will influence the value he awards the act of negotiating, as either a high value activity or a low value activity.

The end result of all these influences will manifest in the distinctions he will make. Fine distinctions and clear goals result from high task value, empowering beliefs and a strong role identity. Coarse distinctions and fuzzy goals result from low task value, limiting beliefs and a weak role identity. The distinctions he makes will decide his choice of behavior.

To further help your understanding of this dynamic, I will invite you into my garden to observe my attempt at cutting the lawn. You can tell by looking at the grass, whether it has been cut by me or by my wife who is the gardener in our family. I have no identity as a gardener, and my goal is usually about how quickly I am able to finish so I can get on with something more important like writing, reading or a family leisure activity. I believe that there is more enjoyment and productivity to be gained from writing than there is from cutting the grass. The result is that I make very coarse distinctions like "have I done this bit?" Even though I have sufficient knowledge to do a good job, I usually make a hash of it.

My wife on the other hand makes much finer distinctions about the height of the mower blades, the thin patches, the curve of the edges, the varying shades of green etc. These finer distinctions are generated from a gardener (identity) who *values* being able to spend time cutting the grass because she *believes* it must be carefully maintained.

Distinctions and goals are comparators that tell us how close we are to achieving a goal. There is a process of continual comparison between distinctions and goals: for example, the *goal* is to finish cutting the entire lawn in 20 minutes, and my "distinctions" are around the time on my wristwatch and the amount of grass remaining to be cut.

My wife's goal on the other hand is to trim the grass by half an inch, smooth the rounded edges and decide whether the thin patches are responding to treatment. Her distinctions are around the length of grass, state of the edges and changes in the thin patches since they were last treated. These finer distinctions drive the behavior that results in a professional job being done in contrast to my quite amateur effort.

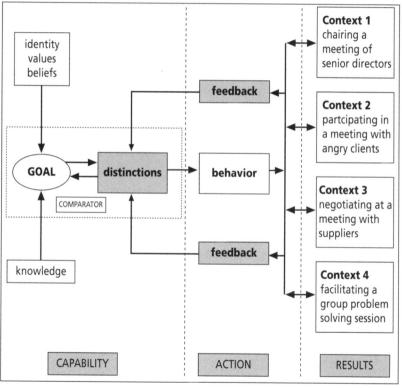

■ FIGURE 1.2
Capability

Much conventional learning restricts flexibility by providing you only with the *knowledge* and *behavior* for a particular context. This is a very basic and attenuated way of learning as it does little to encourage finer micro-distinctions. Figure 1.2 shows four types of meeting. For each meeting type (or context) there will be a specific set of learned behaviors resulting from a mix of training, practical experience and knowledge.

Benjamin Franklin once said "the eye of a master will do more work than both his hands." Ultimate flexibility will be realized when you begin to notice and respond to behavioral patterns and processes.

When it comes to human communication, in any context, there are many finer micro-distinctions that can be made, and it is with these that flexibility can take a quantum leap. A more flexible approach to managing all these situations is to become competent at noticing and responding to the process of human communication rather than content, regardless of the context. Benjamin Franklin once said "the eye of a master will do more work than both his hands." Ultimate flexibility will be realized when you begin to notice and respond to behavioral patterns and processes rather than merely applying a set of learned behaviors to a respective context.

Referring to the generative model in the Introduction, if you are gathering feedback, making fine distinctions and modifying how you operate, context is irrelevant. Let me give you an example from my own experience to demonstrate this point. I remember attending a training course many years ago entitled "effective meetings." On this course I learned about agendas, minutes, keeping to the point, maintaining direction, keeping people focussed on the issues, managing digressions and using visual aids. We did some exercises and role plays to practice the behaviors we were being taught.

When I began to use these new behaviors in meetings at work I hit an enormous problem. The culture in the company at that time could be described in part as being very exciting and dynamic with a great deal of social dialog and interaction mixed with business. It was, and still is, a very young company. Meetings with senior managers and directors often consisted of a half hour exchanging stories about car incidents, office romances and other social escapades. Business was usually left with little time for discussion, and decisions were often made quickly from gut feel and experience.

This is a very successful company, and one that is fun to work in. At a divisional meeting, what reaction do you think I got to the structural response I learned on my course "we seem to be digressing – perhaps a restatement of the meeting objectives might help to keep us focussed on our objectives?"

It didn't go down too well. In fact it damaged the rapport I had built up with some of the managers there. You see it was *important* for people to spend some time talking about social interests – gossiping really! Armed with the right stories, you could get anything

approved – all you needed to do was waste as much time as was necessary to result in a quick decision having to be made. If you rely on
pre-taught contextual structures you are limiting your chances of
success.

The amount of time managers waste in learning contextual structures and behaviors for different aspects of their job is indicative of
the amount of inflexible learning which is available from the myriad
of "management development" courses on the market today. Every
situation is different because people are different and situations
change, so be flexible enough to change your behavior in response to
the feedback you are getting. By doing so you are constantly realigning behind your goals, and reappraising the relevance of your goals
– that is generative development.

■ Behavior – *what?*

Behavior is what you *do* and *say* and it is relatively easy to learn.
Unfortunately some people learn behaviors that hinder rather than
help them achieve their goals. We learn a great many of our behaviors from the significant role models around us. As new-born babies
we learn to smile and say our first words by copying our parents. If
you are lucky you will have a good role model as your manager.

Some people have poor role models from which to learn. I knew
a general manager who many described as authoritarian and dictatorial because of the way he imposed his opinions and decisions onto
others. His voice was pitched in a way that emphasized urgency and
the words came out rather rapidly and sometimes a little confusing.
All decisions had to be made now and there was never enough time
for rational discussion. I found it quite uncanny to observe two of his
closest managers displaying those very same characteristics with a
high degree of precision and accuracy.

■ Environment – *where? when?*

The environment you choose for yourself will determine the quantity and the quality of opportunities from which to get feedback.
Environment is heavily influenced by all the other levels. If you have
a value and belief system that supports being self-sufficient and
spending lots of time by yourself, you will make decisions based on

If you rely on pre-taught contextual structures you are limiting your chances of success.

the avoidance of groups and crowds. This will influence the external situations which will be presented to you.

Managers who consider themselves, above all else, to be administrators generally have to work hard at being people managers because they often prefer to be alone in their office checking and designing administration systems rather than interacting with people. If an office-bound administrator decided to improve his or her people management skills, that person would find it helpful to change their working environment so that they could interact with people more directly and more often. Your environment determines what information is available for you to take in through each of your five senses – sight, hearing, feeling, smell and taste.

The five levels influence each other. If you make a change at one level, all levels below it will also change, although levels above may or may not. Making a change to your identity for example will effect change at all the other four levels below it. Changing your environment may or may not bring about change at other levels above it. When I had decided to take on the *identity* of a developer, I very quickly adopted the *values* and *beliefs* that caused me to discover NLP and I took myself to *environments* where I could learn NLP and enhance my *capabilities* as a developer regardless of the development context.

All around me I see managers struggling to maintain performance levels because they have not yet identified with the roles they need to have that will get them to do the appropriate things. The young-blood who thinks of himself as a problem solver and decision maker will never be a developer and coach until his thinking at the identity level changes. The seasoned manager who thinks of herself as a repository of experience about what can and can't be done in the organization will struggle to develop creative ideas until her thinking at the level of identity changes. The corporate strategist who thinks he has to come up with all the ideas will find it difficult to get others to buy into them until his thinking at the level of identity changes.

Developing a high level of behavioral flexibility requires alignment of the learning levels to each of your goals and roles. It also takes a change of emphasis from noticing only the content of a communication to noticing the process also. Focussing on process will improve responses from *defeat* to *curiosity*, and will begin the journey of unlearning your unhelpful and habitual responses. Success begins with self-awareness, flexibility of thinking and the knowledge that you have choice over how you use, or program, your neurology.

Experience is not what happens to a man. It is what a man does with what happens to him.
Aldous Huxley
(1894–1963)
British novelist and essayist

IDEAS INTO ACTION

- **Common components of communication systems**

- **Models of the world**

- **How the NLP model of communication works**

- **The information filters**

- **Physiology**

Language / Memory / Time / Congruency /
Optimum physiologies

Man does not see the real world. The real world is hidden from him by the wall of imagination.

<small>GEORGE GURDJIEFF</small>
(1874–49)
Russian mystic and author

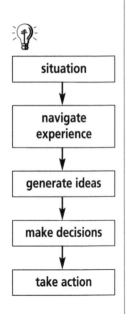

Have you noticed how some managers seem to have the right ideas which are turned into the right kind of action to get desired results? The process has five stages:

- engaging in a situation;
- navigating existing experience;
- generating ideas;
- making decisions;
- taking action.

This is a vital area of management capability, yet so many seemingly brilliant ideas never develop to their expected potential, mainly owing to perceived problems in one or more of the three areas between *situation* and *action*. Whole industries have emerged to solve these types of problem. The number of organizations employing consultants to install quality programs, action teams, re-engineering know-how, and a host of other similar methodologies in the name of "improvement" is a testament to the fact that the average company employee needs help to *navigate experience*, *generate ideas* and *make decisions*.

A favorite analogy of mine is taken from Star Trek (this television series contains exaggerations of many of our human traits), and I draw upon Mr Spock and his Vulcan species to demonstrate a point. Can you imagine what organizational life would be like if we were all Vulcans? We would identify a problem and apply logic to reach a solution. If this were reality – logic without emotions and creative thought, life would be very accurate and precise but unbearably tedious and boring. So we can be thankful for our human attributes of creativity and emotion.

Yet these very same attributes that add spice to our lives are also responsible for much of the disharmony in the human race. The neurological processes that produce creative ideas and generate emotional states are a fundamental part of our complex communication system. To further explain how these attributes affect the generation of ideas, I will now turn to a second analogy – magic.

Do you know the principle by which magicians are able to astound you with the disappearing coin trick? It is based upon perception and sleight of hand. First of all the magician shows you the coin moving from one hand to the other rather quickly. When you have followed his movements doing this a couple of times you have begun to form a habit of observation based upon expectations.

The third time the magician does something slightly different and even more quickly with the result that you miss it completely because you were watching for something else you had been set up for. There is no magic, only magicians and people's perceptions. We are extremely good at forming incorrect perceptions of reality.

Magic exists because of our ability to filter information from our environment and form unique perceptions of reality. So what does this have to do with ideas into action? If our perceptions lead to inappropriate ideas and ineffective decisions, we should expect to be disappointed with our results. If we allow garbage to enter our mind, then we will put garbage back out. Making decisions based on what we think is happening will lead to disappointment. If you are going to develop your sophisticated communication system so that your ideas and decisions are derived from the best quality information available, then you must have a reasonable understanding of the mechanism of human communication. This mechanism is our neurology – a system that is very good at making assumptions, forming incorrect perceptions, jumping to the wrong conclusions and totally misinterpreting the clearest of messages.

The objective of this chapter is to provide a thorough explanation, using the NLP model of communication, of how we (mis)communicate. In chapter 1 you were introduced to some important aspects of communicating with yourself at the level of identity, values and beliefs. In this chapter I will add more elements of your neurology to the communication system, but first it is useful to identify the components which are common to all communication systems.

There is no magic, only magicians and people's perceptions.

Magic exists because of our ability to filter information from our environment and form unique perceptions of reality.

Common components of communication systems

Figure 2.1 shows an information processor connected to a communication system consisting of an encoder, transmitter, a receiver and a decoder to add meaning to information being received.

FIG. 2.1

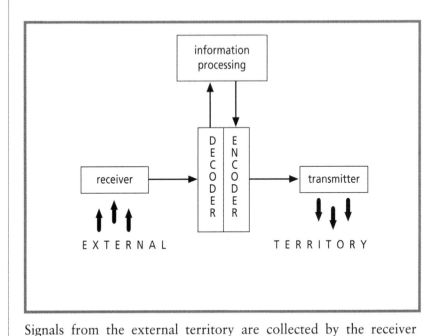

■ FIGURE 2.1
Common
components of
communication
systems

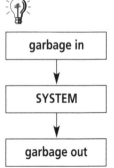

Signals from the external territory are collected by the receiver which passes them on to the decoder. The decoder will only be able to decode information that conforms to the code it is programed with – anything else it will filter out. The decoded information is then sent for processing. Processed information is sent to the encoder to be coded into signals that recipients will identify as information. The code is sent to the transmitter for output to the external territory. This, in essence, is how any communication system works, and it is subject to the universal rule of communication – GIGO (Garbage In Garbage Out). One of the main constraints of this, or any system, is that it is only able to decode signals which it has been programed to recognize – a standard telephone is unable to transmit information contained on a sheet of paper because it is designed to recognize sound. You need an additional decoder such as a fax machine or a personal computer, scanner and modem to achieve this. This simple example is useful in helping to understand the human system of communication – our perceptual filters program our encoders and decoders.

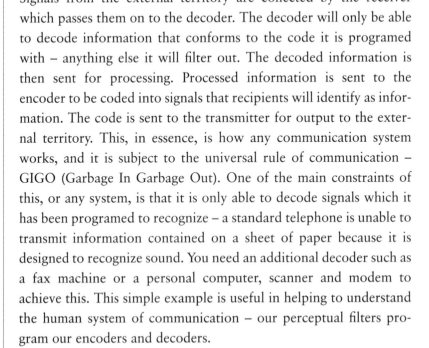

Our perceptual
filters program our
encoders and
decoders.

Models of the world

If you were to consider all the information bombarding our senses at any one moment you could identify up to two million individual pieces. Research and tests have shown that we are only able to consciously pay attention to seven plus or minus two bits of information.[1] In order to make sense of the world around us (the territory) we filter out a great deal of information which we consider unnecessary. Can you imagine what a policeman and an architect might each notice and pay attention to as they walked down a busy city street? I doubt they would have the same experience even if they were walking together as friends. The information we take in, after it has been filtered, forms our own individual map of reality which does not necessarily represent the territory from which we gathered the information to construct our map.

A road map is not the same as the territory. It is but one snapshot in time and does not represent reality. Road maps exclude things like road works, weather, people etc. A territory is always much more detailed than any map created to represent it. Our personal maps contain our assumptions, perceptions, beliefs and values. We use this map to guide our behavior, so it is important to understand when and how we may be filtering information. Have you ever sat in a seminar taking notes to find that you missed what the speaker was saying? In this example the speaker's words are deleted by your filters as conscious attention is directed to writing. Figure 2.2 is a simplified version of the NLP communication model which I will use to help you discover more about how you communicate, generate ideas, make decisions and produce behavior (or actions).

I will first explain the mechanism of the model to give you an overall understanding of how it works and then provide some practical examples to explain each individual element. Later on in this chapter I will introduce you to one of the most simple and effective of all the NLP techniques – the Swish pattern. At this stage we are still working at increasing your awareness of how you generate thought processes and turn these into actions. Once you have this firmly under your grasp, the many techniques and exercises included in this and subsequent chapters will help you to increase your behavioral choice (flexibility), regardless of the context.

[1] Miller G, *The magic number seven plus or minus two*, 1956.

A road map is not the same as the territory. It is but one snapshot in time and does not represent reality.

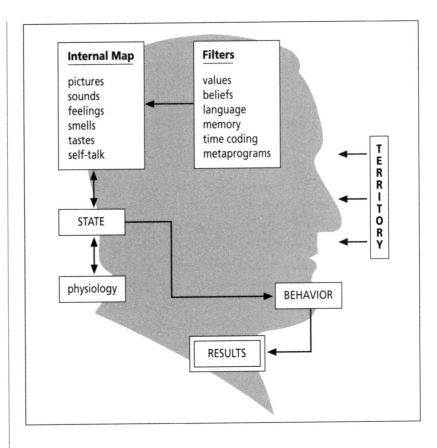

■ FIGURE 2.2
The NLP model of
communication

We actively and
unconsciously seek
out information to
support the things
that are important
to us.

How the NLP model of communication works

We exist in our external environment, or territory, by selecting information through our senses of sight, hearing, smell, taste and touch. Our senses, or our receivers, are bombarded by over two million pieces of information at any one time, and in order to make sense of all this we have to decide which pieces of information we are going to pay attention to. The filters we use to decide what is important and what is unimportant are values, beliefs, memories, language, perception of time and something called "metaprograms" which are habitual filters (metaprograms will be covered later in chapter 4).

Filtered information forms an internal map in the mind by a combination of pictures, sounds, feelings, smells and tastes. Our internal map and our physiology together create a *state of being*. We sometimes talk about being in a particular "state of mind" but we can often be unaware of how much our body contributes to the state. Try getting into a "sad state" while standing up tall with your head held high and a smile across your face – it's extremely difficult. A state of relaxation can be achieved by breathing slowly and deeply and releasing muscle tension.

Our state influences our behavior and so determines the results we get. All behavior is therefore state dependent. This is the process which generates ideas and turns them into action. So increasing behavioral flexibility starts with learning to control states of mind and body, and this requires an understanding of how the information filters work.

The information filters

Values and beliefs cause us to look and listen for information to support what is important to us, and in doing so we overlook a great deal of information which could be useful. We have already discovered how values and beliefs create limitations in each of the roles that make up our identity, so I shall continue this section with *language*.

■ Language

If, through language, we were to give exact representations of our experience, can you imagine what boring and pedantic conversations we would have? You may know some people who are like this. By our use of language we generalize, distort and delete much information from our original experience.

A common example of this is where a colleague returns from a meeting and you ask "how was the meeting?" A typical response to this type of question might be . . . "oh, it was really productive, it took a while to get our minds around some of the issues but we got there eventually". What does this tell you about the meeting? Very little. If you wanted a more accurate account you would need to review the meeting minutes, and even this record of events might include some misinterpretations as a result of words being changed or misplaced.

Words give a very poor and over-simplified account of an original experience, and they are often the cause of much wasted effort. Do you remember the manager who was asked to develop a central IT

Internal representation systems:

V – pictures (visual)
A – sounds (auditory)
K – feelings (kinesthetic)
O – smells (olfactory)
G – tastes (gustatory)

All behavior is state dependent.

Through our use of language we generalize, distort and delete much information from our original experience.

support facility? All that wasted time and effort, not to mention the inconvenience to the people he employed, because he took the language at face value and accepted all the presuppositions contained within it.

We add meaning to the world around us by the use of language which is often not a true representation of our experience. Try this simple teaser as an example:

> *Question:* *The signalman saw the train driver passing a red stop light, but he didn't report this – why?*

Try and come up with your own answer before reading any further.

Answer 1: *The red light was to warn trains going in the opposite direction.*

Answer 2: *The train driver was walking.*

Answer 3: *The signalman was watching a film of the train driver on television.*

Answer 4: *The red light was a road traffic light halting vehicles at a rail crossing point.*

Answer 5: *The signalman was observing the train driver from an airplane which was just taking off over the railway lines.*

Language is the universal code we use to exchange information with other humans. The example above demonstrates how easy it is for us to form unhelpful perceptions of reality by decoding words to mean something completely different from what the originator intended. In order to avoid these mistakes, in this example, you would have to ask these questions:

- *How* specifically did the signalman *see* the train driver?
- *How* exactly was the train driver *passing* the red light?
- *Which* red light, and *where* exactly was it in relation to the train driver and the signalman?

Politicians are extremely good at using language to their advantage. Once you realize how language acts as a filter on experience to create a unique reality for each person, you will begin to appreciate one of the major reasons for communication breakdowns in organizations. In chapter eight I will be introducing you to two language models – the Milton Model, and its antidote, the Meta Model. These models will arm you with the tools to uncover the deeper structure of experience and avoid the traps set by our language.

■ Memory

Memories help to make sense of new information by searching for a link to something which we already know. This process of searching our memory for links to our experience creates expectations for the future. A memory of an experience will contain conditions which influence your thinking and behavior the next time you experience a similar situation: for example, a written request to a senior manager for extra resources may be rejected, and the memory you keep of this rejection will influence how you approach requesting extra resources again in the future. Experiences become generalized to the same meaning for future events of a similar nature.

Emotions are closely linked to memories. Each memory of an experience will contain contextual elements (what, who, where etc.) plus the emotions connected with the experience. When you recall a memory which has a strong emotion attached it is possible to access and actually feel the same feelings which were generated at the time of the original experience. NLP makes use of the link between memory, emotions and feelings by helping to exercise choice over your *state of being*. Some remembered states of being have negative emotions connected to them. These states are called unresourceful states because they inhibit access to many of your internal resources such as logical thought, creativity, confidence, conceptualization etc.

A personnel manager once held a painful memory of a first meeting with a general manager whose manner she interpreted as aggressive and dismissive. This encounter led to her feeling intimidated, and whenever she was faced with attending a future meeting she would recall this first experience and prepare for a similar unpleasant encounter by getting into the remembered unresourceful state of

Once you realize how language acts as a filter on experience to create a unique reality for each person, you will begin to appreciate one of the major reasons for communication breakdowns in organizations.

Each memory of an experience will contain contextual elements (what, who, where etc) plus the emotions connected with the experience.

being. Her memory of the first experience set expectations for all subsequent meetings. Let's run this scenario through the NLP model of communication in figure 2.2 using fictitious names for the two characters involved:

> *Jane (the personnel manager) receives a telephone call from Adrian (the general manager). Adrian speaks very quickly, with a low pitch and sense of urgency in the tone (in music this latter attribute is aptly called "attack"). On hearing Adrian's voice Jane recalls from memory the first meeting she had with Adrian where she felt intimidated – the feeling is very strongly connected in memory to this first experience, particularly to the vocal qualities. The feeling calls up beliefs that she has built around this experience which are reinforced by her internal dialogue: "I don't know how to handle Adrian . . . he's out to undermine my authority . . . he's much more articulate and assertive than me".*

This language has a disempowering influence at the unconscious level. These beliefs support values – "what's important here is to survive the meeting unscathed and without losing credibility". The result of this telephone conversation with Adrian is an internal representation, or map, consisting of visuals, sounds, feelings and any smells or tastes that she may also have connected to this memory. This "map" is how Jane internally represents the experience of the telephone call with Adrian. The map creates a state of general unresourcefulness which affects her physiology (body slumping slightly, some muscles around the shoulders, face and hands tightening).

This mind and body state of being now drives Jane's behavior – what she does and what she says. The result of this is exactly as she anticipated and had prepared for – Adrian gets things all his own way and Jane survives unscathed to do battle another day.

If, like Jane, you hold memories attached to unresourceful emotional states, why not change the memory in some way so that future experiences turn out to be more useful for you. What's the point in re-running old patterns from your memory that get in the way of improving your operational performance? Your ability to generate creative, useful and purposeful ideas will be greatly enhanced by the control you have over your "states of being" in response to feedback from the external territory, and your own neurology. Before I introduce you to a technique to help state control, I will explain the two basic types of state which can be utilized intentionally for different purposes – *associated* and *dissociated*.

Associated state

When you recall an experience from memory, or create an imaginary experience where you are part of the visual representation, you are "associated" to the experience. It is as if you are seeing with your own eyes and hearing with your own ears. Associated states connect you to the feelings, or emotions which are linked to the memory or the created experience. Actors "associate" with their roles to create *real* feelings rather than simulated emotional states. Whenever you want to access a particular feeling, associate with a memory of a time when you last had the feeling.

Dissociated state

When you create a picture in your mind's eye, of a memory or an imaginary situation, and where you are observing yourself, you are "dissociated" from the experience. Dissociating removes emotional content from the experience. This technique is used by therapists when they want their subjects to recreate a traumatic experience without re-experiencing the emotional content. The Swish technique uses a dissociated imaginary representation to change an unresourceful state to a resourceful one. I will introduce you to it using the visual system as this is the easiest for most people, although some may find working in the kinesthetic or auditory systems preferable.

The Swish pattern

 EXERCISE 3

Step 1

Recall an interaction where you responded in a way that generates concern as you think about it now. It could be a meeting, a telephone call or a presentation – any interaction where you would like to change future responses from unresourceful to resourceful.

Your ability to generate creative, useful and purposeful ideas will be greatly enhanced by the control you have over your "states of being."

Step 2

Find the trigger to the unresourceful state. How do you know when to create the state for yourself? In the Jane /Adrian example, Jane's state was triggered by a picture she created in her mind as she thought of Adrian. Her state became worse as she added Adrian's voice to her internally represented picture of Adrian speaking to her on the telephone. This is an internal trigger (created entirely in the mind). At other times the trigger would come from Adrian's voice over the telephone (external trigger). If, in your example, the trigger is an internal representation, then reconstruct the visual, auditory, olfactory, and gustatory elements just as they normally occur in your mind. If the trigger is external, then use all modalities to create a fully associated internal representation, i.e. as if you are re-experiencing the memory.

Step 3

Identify two qualities of your internal picture that, when intensified, change your internal response to it. Usually brightness and size are qualities that work well, but color, contrast, location or depth may work also. You will probably notice the internal response as a feeling or emotion. Play around with this until you are happy with the two chosen qualities. These qualities (called submodalities) are the "critical submodalities."

Step 4

Now stand up, walk around and think of something completely different for a few moments. This gets you to break out of the state you have just thought yourself into.

Dissociated pictures create the motivation to move towards something you want.

Step 5

Construct a new image of how you would rather be in response to this interaction. The image you create is of a different you, having the resources now to choose a better outcome. This different you is moving towards the person you want to be in this situation. Your picture must be dissociated, that is – you are looking at yourself in the picture. Dissociated pictures create the motivation to move towards something you want. An associated picture would give you the feeling that you already had the resources, so make it dissociated.

Make sure that you include all the resources you need. Resources might include assertiveness, confidence, clarity of thought, listening ability, creativity, questioning ability etc. Choose your own resources – if you choose skills, make sure you have at least a knowledge of the skill – if you need a skill which you don't have yet then find a way of acquiring the skill as soon as possible.

Your image needs to be compelling and realistic. It also needs to be checked out with respect to other areas of your personality and relationships. Try it out for different contexts – is this new *you* compatible with other relationships? If you were to respond in this way in different contexts, would the outcome be favorable to you and those you interact with? You may want to alter the image until you are entirely happy with it.

Step 6

Now go for another walk around the room and think about something entirely different for a few moments – this is a "state breaker" – the same as in Step 4.

Step 7

Take your first image and intensify the critical submodalities – as in Step 3. Now take your new self-image, make it small and dark and put it in a corner of your first image. The next step requires speed. As you say to yourself "swish" or "swoosh," instantaneously make the large picture small and dark while making the new self-image large and bright.

Step 8

Repeat Step 7 about five times, making sure that you "break state" between each one. Speed and repetition are essential.

Step 9

To test your new "response" all you need to do is trigger the state again by imagining a future time when you will want this different response. This is called "future pacing." If your trigger is external all you have to do is imagine the event that would trigger your state. If you still get the original response go back to Step 1 and do it again, although by the time you have "swished" your images five to six times you will find that the new state swishes itself.

"Swish" the critical submodalities (brightness and size work well for many people)

■ FIGURE 2.3
The Swish

I encourage you to experiment with this technique and use it often. You can exert more choice over your internal maps of reality by programing your neurology to respond to the external territory in more resourceful ways. This way your perceptual filters are working to improve and enhance how you operate, removing self-imposed limitations.

■ Time

It isn't possible to manage time; what you actually do is manage yourself *in* and *through* time.

The modern concept of time management is a fallacy. It isn't possible to manage time; what you actually do is manage yourself *in* and *through* time. Imagine what answers you might get if you were to ask ten people selected at random what they were doing two weeks ago last Tuesday. Are you likely to get the same answers? Of course not. The answers you might get will vary from "I don't know" to "I think I was . . ." and "yes, I was playing tennis with my girlfriend" or something similarly specific. Follow this by asking them what they will be doing precisely three weeks from now. Some will be able to tell you exactly what they will be doing, others may have a vague idea, and there will be those that haven't given it a thought.

We all have our own way of thinking about time. Some people are good long term planners, other people have difficulty thinking further ahead than the end of the week. Our ability to recall past events also varies immensely. The way in which we perceive time internally has a major influence on how we recall past events, experience the now, and plan future events. You might think that time should be the same for everyone – we have clocks and watches to help us conceptualize time into our lives, and they are all synchronized to move at the same speed. NLP provides a technique called "timeline" which can be used to help reorganize unhelpful time perception (or time coding), and to help us make the best use of time by planning our actions in a way that helps to achieve our objectives.

Timeline is a metaphor – and a very useful one. It uses the principle of coding time within and around the physical space our body occupies. It is possible to have time organized as a chronological line going from the past through the present and to the future. I have also come across many people with very different and much more complex configurations than this. However, there are some general principles which have been found to be consistent, and which are useful in helping us to understand the advantages and disadvantages of different types of timeline.

There are two basic forms of timeline, each with many variations. People who seem to live permanently in the here and now will often be late for appointments because the *now* is much more important and real to them than the future. You will find that these people are usually late for meetings because they get totally involved in the *now* and afford little value to time schedules, which they frequently overrun. They are also easily persuaded to stay late when deeply engaged in a discussion. When their attention is focussed they are easily able to keep it that way.

These people tend not to work with personal organizers, often preferring simple diary entries to record future events. Living *in-time* creates memories with high emotional content which, when recalled, are usually fully associated experiences. People who are "in-time" generally have timeline configurations similar to those shown in figure 2.4. (A-B; X-Y) where the body is actually "in" the timeline.

The way in which we perceive time internally has a major influence on how we recall past events, experience the now, and plan future events.

Living *in-time* creates memories with high emotional content which, when recalled, are usually fully associated experiences.

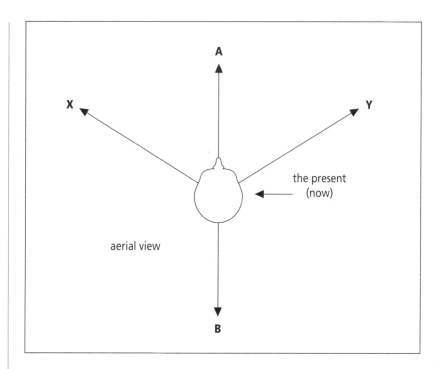

A

X

Y

the present
(now)

aerial view

B

If you can
determine your
own timeline you
can also change it,
and use it as a
highly effective
planning system to
help you plan for
success.

The second basic timeline configuration is *through-time* as shown in Figure 2.5. People who have their timelines configured in this way are more likely to use complex personal organizer systems because the past and future have as much importance as the now. These people often become distracted by their own thoughts of other events in the past and future, and even though they are with you in body, their minds can often be elsewhere. They will usually be consistently on time to most appointments and extreme *through-time* people may actually arrive up to an hour early as being late is totally unimaginable to them, and being on time is often more important than the meeting itself.

These two basic configurations are typical for right-handed people. Left-handed people may find the past and future reversed in lateral configurations.

Where is your timeline? Are you in-time or through-time? How do you perceive or code time in relation to the physical space in and around your body? If you can determine your own timeline you can also change it, and use it as a highly effective planning system to help you plan for success.

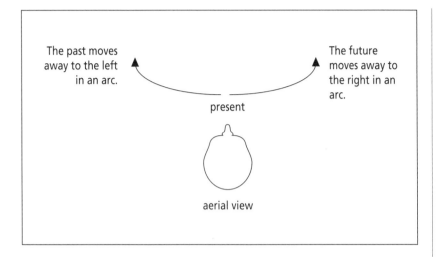

The past moves away to the left in an arc.

The future moves away to the right in an arc.

present

aerial view

■ FIGURE 2.5
A typical "through-time" timeline configuration

To elicit your own configuration, pick a time from your distant past when you were celebrating a birthday, and recall some specific experiences from the day. Now think of another birthday a few years later than that one, and do the same. Now think of another birthday a few years later . . . and keep going until you get to your most recent birthday. Stay with each memory for a few moments, bringing to mind as many images as possible from each birthday.

Now I want you to go through this process again, and this time see if you can locate from which direction the internal images of you celebrating your birthday are coming from. Draw an imaginary line through each image and you will have your metaphorical timeline. It may not be like either of the two examples shown in figures 2.4 and 2.5 – that's alright. There are people with very peculiar configurations indeed. Some Asian cultures have vertical up/down timelines, and I know some people with spirals around their body. The point is, how useful is your timeline in its present form? If it's not very useful then imagine how you would prefer it to be. How effective are you at finishing work on time? How about investing your time, do you invest it wisely? Is your general time-keeping OK? Can you confidently plan major important projects years in advance? How about day-to-day time investment and general time discipline?

If you want to improve in any of these areas it may be worth experimenting with alternative timelines. The one which is most suited to western business is the "front v-shaped through-time" timeline (as shown in figure 2.5). In chapter 5 you will have the opportunity of using your timeline to plan for a successful future event.

Physiology

At this stage it is important to introduce physiology because of the huge impact it has on everything you think and do. Referring to the NLP communication model (figure 2.2), the mind and body are one system and therefore influence each other. The result of their influence on each other is a *state of being*, and this state determines your behavior. Have you ever found yourself lacking the drive to get something done because you are in *the wrong state of mind*? Or sometimes because you just don't feel like doing something. How is your state affected by what your mind is thinking and what your body is feeling? What state of mind and body do you need to be in to get something done? It is clear that certain tasks require a particular state, and that the state is a combination of how the mind and body are influencing each other.

■ Congruency

Physiology includes posture, movement, expression, gesture, breathing, muscle tone, external touch and internal feelings. Try this from a standing position. Slump forward, put on a sad face, let your knees bend, drop your shoulders, slow your breathing down, let your eyelids droop, let all your muscles sag and say . . . "I'm feeling on top of the world today." How did that feel? Peculiar? Would you expect anyone to believe you?

What you did was to give your brain a signal that you were feeling tired or deflated and so the words that you said came out with an incongruency to the message your body was giving. You generated a mixed message. You would not expect to deliver a brilliant corporate presentation if your body and mind were not in complete harmony with one another. It's no good standing in a confident posture if your internal dialog is saying "I'm too nervous to do this – I haven't had enough experience." You will not be at your best if you are incon-

Many of your "gut feelings" are unconscious signals of incongruency. Listen to them, they are offering you feedback.

gruent in any way. If your boss asks you if you want a promotion and you answer yes, but with a waver in your voice and a hunched posture – you need to find out why you have incongruent signals.

Often, the unconscious will send signals of incongruency via mind or body because it has identified a problem area. Could the unconscious have concerns about the ecology of hasty decisions? Many of your "gut feelings" are unconscious signals of incongruency. Listen to them, they are offering you feedback.

■ Optimum physiologies

For any task there is an optimum physiology that will add congruency to your state of being and enhance your operation. Getting feedback from inside about how you feel is just as important as the feedback you get from the external territory. If you are in a meeting with senior managers and you suddenly get a feeling of being cut out of the discussion – this is feedback. Where is the feeling, and how has it affected your overall state?

You need to adjust your physiology in some way – how are you breathing? High in the chest or from the stomach? Fast or slow? Breathe differently and check your state. How are you holding your body? Are your muscles tensed? Are you leaning to one side? Are you rigid or slightly slumped? Make some changes and check your state again. You don't need drastic changes, small changes are usually enough to alter your state. And remember to check what's going on in your mind also. What are your perceptual filters doing? How useful is your internal dialogue at this time? What changes do you need to make to become fully congruent with yourself right now?

If you're going to make a valid contribution to the meeting you need to do it with congruence and confidence. Any incongruence will be noticed by the others and processed by their own perceptual filters, so who knows how they are going to represent you inside their own minds. I will be returning to physiology and congruency signals in sections two and three as you discover how to use your physiology to build rapport, influence other people and develop personal impact.

We are never deceived; we deceive ourselves.

JOHANN WOLFGANG VON GOETHE (1749–1832)
German poet, dramatist, novelist

Any incongruence will be noticed by the others and processed by their own perceptual filters.

CREATING DIRECTION

■ **Commitment**

Describing present state and desired state / Designing your
direction / Making it happen

**The music the
orchestra hears is
not the music the
audience hears.**

Commitment

There are probably more metaphors in management theory for direction than for anything else. The idea behind creating direction is to harness the full potential of the workforce and achieve the elusive 110 percent effort. This is the ultimate in getting the most out of people – creating an environment in which people are fully committed to achieving business objectives as a result of intrinsic motivation rather than some external carrot or stick approach.

One of my favorite metaphors is the orchestra which consists of a group of people highly skilled in musicianship and where each individual has a particular talent for producing music from one or more instruments. Together, given the same music scores, they can interpret complex musical notation, translate it into physical action as they connect with their instruments, and make sounds that stir the emotions of the listener. So what does the conductor do? He provides direction in many ways. Imagine you are the trumpet player in a 50-piece orchestra. Do you think you could hear the flutes over the percussion? The music the orchestra hears is not the music the audience hears. A listener sitting in the audience front left will hear different music than a listener sitting back right.

Now imagine you're in the orchestra watching an inspirational conductor – the body movements that keep time, co-ordinate and synchronize the different sections; gestures to recognize your contribution and lead you to high peaks and soft undertones; driving emotion into the music with great sweeping emphasis from highly visual physiological signals. This is direction. Enthusiasts of orchestral music can often tell you the name of a conductor by listening to the music and recognizing their particular style. Not all conductors direct in the same way, but without direction you lose emotional content which is what music is all about.

As a manager you can allow your experts to follow instructions in your written memos, and they will always find enough work to fill their time and be productive. The big question is for all managers is "how do you create an environment that stimulates intrinsic motivation so that people are committed to contributing 110 percent?"

First of all you must know what direction is the right one. Then you need to be personally 110 percent committed to the direction yourself – with the passion of an inspirational conductor.

This chapter offers you a three stage model for creating direction for your team, aligning yourself to the direction, and creating the right neurological conditions that will help you to "make it happen." The model (figure 3.1) can be thought of as providing the feedback from a high level of organizational mission with which to align your energy and begin to direct the energy of your team. This model of direction concentrates on providing feedback for you so that you are able to be a passionate and committed role model for your team. How you translate the direction into team action will be covered in section 2 – leadership.

You need to be personally 110 percent committed to the direction yourself – with the passion of an inspirational conductor.

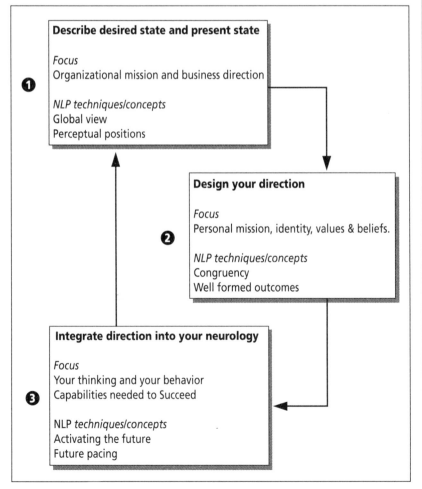

Describe desired state and present state

Focus
Organizational mission and business direction

NLP techniques/concepts
Global view
Perceptual positions

❶

Design your direction

Focus
Personal mission, identity, values & beliefs.

NLP techniques/concepts
Congruency
Well formed outcomes

❷

Integrate direction into your neurology

Focus
Your thinking and your behavior
Capabilities needed to Succeed

NLP techniques/concepts
Activating the future
Future pacing

❸

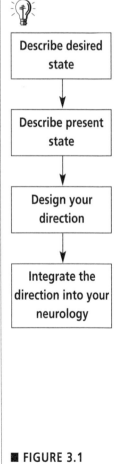

Describe desired state

↓

Describe present state

↓

Design your direction

↓

Integrate the direction into your neurology

■ FIGURE 3.1
Creating direction

Here you will be taken through the direction model offering you exercises that build high success potential.

■ Describing present state and desired state

Creating direction implies that you desire to be somewhere other than where you are right now. There is a basic human desire that causes us to think in this way. No matter how much we are enjoying our current environment, at some future time we will want some change for ourselves. All organizational improvement processes are based upon this basic desire – to go from the present situation (or state) to some other desired situation (or state) preferably more secure and profitable than at present. So, there is the notion of moving away from where you are, and moving toward some other state which may be known or unknown. It is always best to know where you're going otherwise you could end up anywhere.

It is always best to know where you're going otherwise you could end up anywhere.

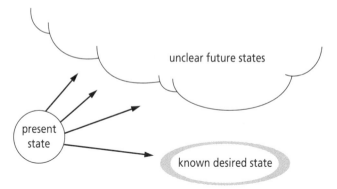

In my experience of providing training in support of organizational development programs I have been able to observe how many times the "goal posts" move from the time of conducting the needs analysis to completing the training design stage. This is indicative of a management that wants to change but is unclear about the desired situation. The result of this pattern is that the future evolves as a sequence of knee-jerk reactions to current events rather than a strategic, planned succession of managed changes. *If you don't know what the future is going to look like, how can you invest in the skills you will need when you get there?*

Global view

To begin to describe your desired state you need to view your part of the organization as a function of the whole organization. If you're a CEO you will want to consider your organization as part of the market it operates in. At this stage you need to think systemically about parts and wholes. What logical larger part of the system is your span of responsibility a part? Do you recall the law of requisite variety in chapter 1? You are about to make your part of the organization the most flexible by creating the direction needed to continually realign behind the larger system's mission and business objectives.

To be successful at this you need the personal flexibility to incorporate all the feedback you will be getting as you create direction for yourself and your team. First, you need to know the higher level mission and objectives, and you will want to put some concrete reality into the generalized words used to build corporate missions. Statements like "we aim to be number one" carry little meaning without concrete realities to back them up. Some organizations are better than others at designing mission statements, transmitting them down the hierarchy and translating them into operational objectives. If you have insufficient information of a global nature to decide the direction for your part of the organization then I strongly suggest that you make this your first outcome.

Many organizations know the direction they are going in but their communication structures block the dissemination of this important information. You may have to be persistent in seeking it out. What *does* the organization expect of you?

What *does* the organization expect of you?

Perceptual positions

In the global system you are part of the orchestra and this perspective limits what you hear. From your current position you are not able to judge how the audience is hearing your music until you stop playing and listen for the strength of applause, or silence (your feedback). This is often the case in organizations – you can become so involved in production or service delivery that it is difficult to tell if your efforts are being channeled in the right direction until you stop and begin activities that will generate useful feedback from your cus-

From your current position you are not able to judge how the audience is hearing your music until you stop playing and listen for the strength of applause, or silence (your feedback).

tomers, both internal and external. Unfortunately, as feedback is subjective, unless you invest time to design a well balanced feedback system, you may find that most of your feedback comes from a small number of customers and therefore does not represent the whole of your customer base.

Whether you are producing goods, delivering a service, or engaging in any type of interaction with another person, your operation is judged by different criteria from different perspectives. A line manager and a company director, for example, will perceive the work of a company accountant differently. The perceptual positions technique helps to gain an insight into multiple perspectives of your own behavior or the way your department, or company operates, by simulating the sound of the music from at least two additional perspectives other than your own.

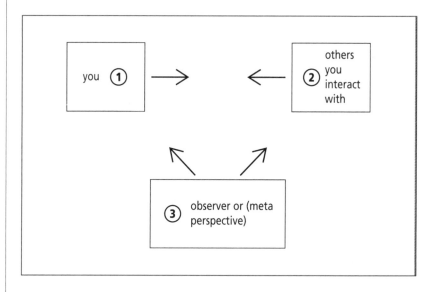

■ FIGURE 3.2
Perceptual positions

Our autopilot is quite capable of thinking about situations from different perspectives, but you get far superior results when this natural activity is carried out with purpose and intention. It's about the quality of your thinking. You may be fortunate enough to get useful feedback from your customers, and this is often the best quality information available to you.

The perceptual positions exercise will allow you to integrate this information as you take on your customer's perspectives. Position 1 is you. Position 2 is your customer's perspective, and there may be multiple perspectives if you have different groups of customers to provide for. Position 3 is an observer perspective, or meta position (meaning sitting over and above everything else). From this meta position you are able to observe the interaction between you and your customers. Here's an exercise to help you use perceptual positions.

Perceptual positions

 **EXERCISE 4**

1 Think of an interaction you have with another person that is uncomfortable, or that puzzles you in some way.

2 Place three markers on the floor, one at each point of a triangle so that they are about six feet from one another. Identify these points as *you*, the *other person* in the interaction, and an *observer*.

3 Stand on *your* marker and look at the *other person*. Answer the question "how does their behavior affect me?" Get some quality information before moving on to the next step.

4 Stand on the *other person's* marker and *become* that person by associating into their role. Look back at your marker and get a feel for what you see and what you hear. Answer the question "what does this behavior do / not do for me?" Get some quality information before proceeding to the next step.

5 Stand on the observer's marker and take a view at both the other markers. Look for what is happening and what is being said. What process is taking place? What is/isn't being achieved? It is important to remain dissociated from both roles as you observe them.

6 Repeat steps 3–5 as many times as it takes for new insights to emerge. Make sure that you "break state" between steps 3 and 5 by thinking of something totally unconnected for a few moments.

This technique can also be used at a departmental or company level. As long as you are able to associate into the second position (or role) you will get some interesting new insights to others' perceptions which may provide answers to puzzling or confusing situations, and help you to create direction for your team. Here's how you could set

Only by really associating into customer roles can you take on their perspectives of your operation.

up multiple second position perspectives for an internal service provider department (refer to figure 3.3).

Position 1   Scope of responsibility for the department, and the department's mission and objectives.

Position 2(a) An employee's perspective of your service.

Position 2(b) A business manager's perspective of your service,

Position 2(c) A board member's perspective of your service.

Position 3   An observer's perspective of each interaction.

In addition to the interactions between position 1 and multiple 2s, notice the interaction between board member, manager and employee. The dynamics between these perspectives are important also. By associating into each second position role, the department manager is able to get a feel for how other roles in the organization perceive the integration of service, provided by his department, into everyday working practices.

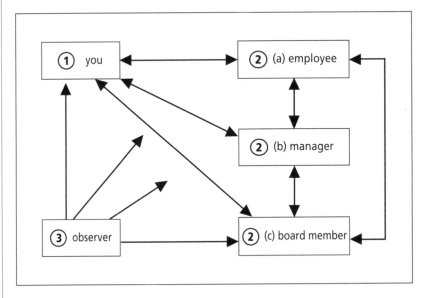

■ FIGURE 3.3
Multiple second position perspectives.

It is not necessary to spatially "mark out" each position on the floor, but this does help to ensure that you "break-state" as you move between positions. It is important to be in a clean, associated, state to help you "become" each of the second position roles. Only by really associating into customer roles can you take on their perspectives of your operation.

You can run through this activity with your team by using role play. Some people can play customer roles while others take the meta position. You will need to keep the team associated into their roles, so it is a good idea to invite a facilitator to help orchestrate this for you. In the section on innovation you will be introduced to a modified version of this exercise which is used to generate creative ideas.

This activity will help you to discover lots of useful ideas for improvements that are customer-focussed. It will help you to "think outside of the departmental square" and help to be more exacting in recognizing what needs to change. It will help you to design the strategy that will guide your team to a desired future state while avoiding the knee-jerk strategy that leads to unclear future states. Some of the feedback I have gained through this exercise I doubt would have come from any other method.

I encourage you to explore perceptual positions either spatially by yourself, or with your team. Alternatively, run it through in your mind (remember to break-state between each position).

■ Designing your direction

Congruence

Following the direction model (refer to figure 3.1) we have arrived at step 2 where your focus needs to be on personal mission, identity, values and beliefs. This is all about becoming a role model for your team. If you expect the team to "buy in" to your directionalizing they will need to see that you are not only congruent in your messages, but that everything you do and say reinforces the way you want them to go. Your orchestra will follow if you lead with enthusiasm and a solid belief in purpose.

In exercise 1 you generated some role labels for your identity, and exercise 2 invited you to check out your values and beliefs around your job role. As you begin to design your new direction, compare your personal values and beliefs with those that need to be in place to support the new direction.

You need to be aligned here. For example, if your feedback suggests that you should be proactively presenting information to large management groups, but your identity, values and beliefs have you marked down as an administrator, you have a major mismatch. How are you going to deal with this? If you value being responsible for a

Design the strategy that will guide your team to a desired future state.

Your orchestra will follow if you lead with enthusiasm and a solid belief in purpose.

Align behind the new direction and become a success model for your people.

highly successful department more than you value being an administrator, you might adopt the belief that the former can only happen if you begin meeting with each management group. You need to align behind the new direction and become a success model for your people.

Well formed outcomes

Over 300 years before Christ, Aristotle wrote:

> "All men seek one goal; success or happiness. The only way to achieve true success is to express yourself completely in service to society. First, have a definite, clear, practical ideal – a goal, an objective. Second, have the necessary means to achieve your ends – wisdom, money, materials and methods. Third, adjust your means to that end".

Well Formed Outcomes
Positively stated
Resourced and realistic
Initiated and maintained by self
Ecological to you and others
Sensory based evidence criteria
Time phased

Having goals and objectives is not a new idea. However, it is more useful to talk about outcomes than objectives because outcomes cover consequences and objectives don't. Remember the chap who set himself an objective of becoming a millionaire? The consequences led to the breakdown of his family. Well formed outcomes could have prevented this situation. So, assuming you have described what the desired state is for your team, it is time to construct outcomes that will get you there, and to help you recall this simple yet extremely effective method I shall use the mnemonic PRIEST.

State your outcomes in the positive.

Positively stated   Take a few moments to not think of a green giraffe. I said to *not* think of a green giraffe. The mind can only represent a negative (not) by making it a positive. If you go around telling people what not to do, don't be surprised when they end up doing precisely what you wanted them to avoid doing.

This is a key factor in parenting and education. I stopped telling my students *not to forget* a long time ago. Remembering is much more conducive to learning, don't you think? The mind converts negatives to positives, so state your outcomes in the positive – what *you want to achieve* rather than what you want to avoid, otherwise you might end up with getting what you don't want. Also, by only stating what you want to avoid, you may find that individual team members begin to design their own future desired states which may not be conducive to the aims of the organization.

Resourced and realistic   Make sure you have, or can acquire all the resources you need to achieve your outcomes. Resources can include physical assets like people, money and materials. The term can also include knowledge and skills. Also, set realistic outcomes. Unrealistic outcomes can have a devastating effect on motivation and may create an environment of high stress.

Initiated and maintained by self   If your outcomes rely on others too much you are asking for trouble. You are responsible for your own part of the business. No-one else is going to bail you out or carry the can if you don't deliver (unless you work in a country club type of company). Ask this question of your outcomes: *do I have sufficient authority and control in the organization to achieve my outcomes without having to rely on other people to make things happen?* If the answer is no, rethink your outcomes and how you are going to achieve them. Your outcomes should be initiated and maintained by you so that you have the flexibility to respond to changes in the system as you begin to move towards them.

Ecological   As you think through what needs to be done to achieve your outcomes, do it with a sensitivity to other parts of the system. What consequences will there be as a result of you moving towards this outcome? Could there be repercussions along the way with other managers, employees, departments, customers, suppliers, family members, and friends? How will they be affected? And how about yourself? Are you completely congruent about what you need to do to achieve this outcome? Listen to your incongruencies – they have a purpose.

Are you completely congruent about what you need to do to achieve this outcome?

Sensory-based evidence criteria   How will you know when you have achieved your outcomes? What evidence criteria will you decide upon? Make it sensory-based evidence – what will you see, hear, feel that will tell you if you have achieved your outcome?

Time phased   Have you time phased your outcomes? Will the time realistically allow everything to get done? When specifically do you expect to achieve your outcomes? Your team will want to know these timescales otherwise you may discover other people's priorities stealing the time you need to achieve *your* outcomes. This subject will be covered in more detail in chapter 5.

Setting outcomes that are well formed is one of NLP's fundamentals. As you think about outcomes, they don't have to be related to long-term desires. You should have an outcome for every action you take, and I will be talking more about this in the section on communication.

■ Making it happen

Let's assume you have involved your team in deciding the desired state, and outcomes have been set. Everything that happens in your department from this point on needs to be aligned behind your outcomes. For example, imagine you are manager of the marketing department of a large oil company and one of your aims is to design and produce, in standard format and on a six monthly basis, worldwide marketing strategy plans for senior business unit directors. You will need to design a system to produce this information, one that incorporates workflow and communication lines to capture information, process it and issue it out to identified receivers.

Figure 3.4 shows this as a basic input/output diagram with a feedback loop. A "total quality" company will have many feedback loops built into their work processes. Thinking of the work in your department systemically, as in figure 3.4, and defining the inputs and outputs to each process, provides you with a basis for checking whether what is actually happening in your department is aligned to your outcomes.

Any malfunction is feedback.

Your feedback system should be designed to give you information about direction and outcomes – are you on the right track? If you suddenly find that information is being formated in a different way from what you had agreed, you have a malfunction in the system. Any malfunction is feedback, so you will want to investigate why there is a deviation from the agreed outcomes. It could be that the system is advising you that new outcomes need to be formed as the business moves on. Be flexible and go back to step 1 of the direction model (Figure 3.1) to check this out. The system input/output diagram is a useful method of assessing how well the energy of your team is directed towards your outcomes, and how appropriate your outcomes are as your customer needs change.

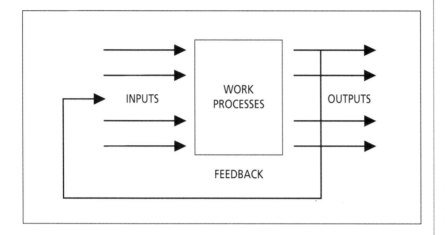

■ FIGURE 3.4
Basic work system diagram

Capabilities

Referring back to the levels of learning and change in chapter 1, you will want to assess your own capabilities and those of your team. This is a feature of setting well formed outcomes and it is an area which, in my experience, often suffers from gross neglect. You may have heard of the "Peter principle" – that people are promoted to their level of incompetence. All you need to do is compare knowledge and skills against the tasks to be done and you have identified the skills gap that needs to be plugged.

Training and developing people into new and more challenging roles has huge payoffs, but then you might expect me to say that, considering my profession. Having the flexibility to continually realign behind outcomes and corporate direction creates an environment of change and variety that provides opportunities to stimulate personal development.

Integration – a vital catalyst

Very often, the ingredients that determine the degree of success in achieving any outcome are intrinsic to a person's neurology. Even with the best thought out plans, with precise detail and instruction at every level, success is often not realized. The human element is so critical.

Imagine two groups of ten year olds. One group is highly enthusiastic and motivated by their teacher who makes learning fun and enjoyable. The second group is stuck with a teacher who talks and chalks all day with a monotone voice and who would rather be somewhere else. Now give each group similar building sets and instructions to build any structure of their choosing. You can imagine the results you would get.

The capabilities of any system consisting of a set of processes or instructions are subject to the mental and physical energy applied by the people working it, and in the same way that teachers are behavioral examples for their pupils, managers are behavioral examples, or role models, for their team in the workplace. If you are not motivated and enthused by the direction you have set, don't expect your people to be either. You need to make the desired future state a compelling place to directionalize your energies, in other words you can *activate the future*.

Activating the future Research to discover what makes entrepreneurs successful shows that very few of them produce detailed plans. They usually have lots of ideas and perhaps some global plans, but the detail is often left to sort itself out. What is common among many successful entrepreneurs is a strategy for visualizing their direction, or outcomes. In 1985 the young chairman of the Virgin Group said:

> "I *see* Virgin *becoming* the largest entertainment group based outside the US. Getting to where we are now was quite difficult. Getting from here to a billion-pound company will be much easier. I sometimes wonder what type of company we'll be *then*."

These words, spoken by Richard Branson, give clues to his internal strategy for success. It is clear that he had visualized getting to be a billion-pound company. His belief structure has determined that he will get there. In his mind he is already doing the things that will achieve this.

The visual modality is very powerful and it can be used to guide our unconscious behavior towards our outcomes. Our mental pictures provide signposts for our behavior, directing us to make the right decisions from day to day that move us in the direction we wish to go.

If you are not motivated and enthused by the direction you have set, don't expect your people to be either.

Our mental pictures provide signposts for our behavior, directing us to make the right decisions from day to day that move us in the direction we wish to go.

It works in a similar way to a computer screen which has been left switched on for a number of years with the same image on screen. Eventually the screen image gets burnt-in to the tube so that you can actually see the image when the screen is turned off. The visualization technique *burns-in* a compelling future to your neurology.

Imagine what you, your team and your customers will be doing and saying when you have achieved your outcomes. Visualize this into a mental picture – make it bright and clear with lots of color. Keep it a dissociated picture – you are looking as an observer. Enlarge it so that you can see the detail of people's faces as they express delight at your products or service. Make your picture 3D and put in movement. Add the sounds you would expect to hear around you, and now intensify all these qualities so that the images burn-in to your mind.

When you have intensified enough you will begin to feel success. It may be a slight flutter in the stomach area, or a confident smile. Your body will begin to take on the posture of success, your head will be up, eyes up, seeing, hearing and feeling a successful future. Have you done this yet? Good, now see yourself doing this regularly to make absolutely sure that you integrate success potential into your whole neurology.

The technique you have just practiced is also a *future pace*. By visualizing success you have imagined what the desired state will be like. It's a bit like trying on the future to see if it fits. If it doesn't fit you will get feedback in some way, probably as a signal of incongruence from some part of your physiology. If this happens you know what to do. Incorporate the feedback, make adjustments to your outcomes and *reactivate*.

Your reason and your passion are the rudder and the sails of your seafaring soul. If either your sails or your rudder be broken, you can but toss and drift, or else be held at a standstill in mid-seas.

K. GIBRAN, The Prophet

SELF MASTERY

■ The sixth strategy

Fear of failure / Identity mismatch / Unclear outcomes / Dislike
of the task / Unskilled / Motivated

*He who knows others is
   clever;
He who knows himself
   has discernment.
He who overcomes
   others has force;
He who overcomes
   himself is strong.*

TAO TE CHING, book one

NLP

*You have all the
resources you need
to succeed. There is
no failure only
feedback.*

I was recently interviewed by a magazine journalist who wanted a story about outdoor training. Her pleasant manner and confident style projected a high level of professionalism. She was also extremely ambitious. We had a very enjoyable lunch together and after the interview she confided in me that her career potential was not being realized because she couldn't bring herself to call top editors with her scoops. Why should an ambitious, confident, capable, intelligent woman procrastinate over something as simple as that?

If you know enough about yourself you can learn how to motivate yourself to do just about anything. Most people however know very little about the unconscious patterns of thought and behavior that help them to decide what to invest energy and resources in, what to procrastinate over, and what to avoid. This chapter analyzes certain personality traits that influence motivation and suggests ways of building extra motivational flexibility through language, thinking patterns and behavior. The outcome is to develop a high degree of flexibility into your thinking and behavior so that you have a sense of mastery over how you operate as a manager within the organization.

There are two major principles to this chapter:

- you have all the resources you need to succeed,
- there is no failure only feedback.

Get these on board into your belief system and all that needs to be done to develop self-mastery is to access and take control of your resources.

The purpose of a human resource department is to manage, develop and utilize each individual's resource for the benefit of both organization and employee aspirations. One of the problems with HR is that in generalizing developmental and motivational initiatives across the whole organization, much individual resource remains dormant through lack of appropriate stimulation. HR departments could be doing more *resource development* to help individuals manage, develop and take responsibility for their own resources and less generalized *resource management*. This chapter seeks to address this resource issue for the individual.

As a manager there will be activities that you excel at, there may be others that you are just learning, and there may be some areas where you would rather not get involved. Regardless of how you see yourself, or how you feel about any particular activity, there will be times when results will depend upon how well you perform a particular task or activity, and before you do anything, you need to motivate yourself to *want* to do it. Any task lacking self-motivation will have a degree of reluctance attached – and reluctance is often an enemy of self-mastery. *Goals* that are not also *wants* are unlikely to be achieved.

The sixth strategy

Why do you do anything? What prevents you from doing some things and what compels you to do others? How is it that you can be intrinsically motivated to complete some tasks superbly well, and not others? I am talking entirely about self-motivation, not external carrot and stick motivation which can be turned on and off by your organization.

As a manager you need the flexibility to motivate yourself at any time, for any task using intrinsic means – regardless of the external attempts of the organization to manipulate your energies. As a role model and example of how to be for your team, creating an image of self-mastery will have a positive influence. Figure 4.1, the sixth strategy shows five strategies for procrastination and one strategy (the sixth) which is a motivation strategy needed for self-mastery.

There are five main reasons why tasks are either unfinished, or finished but to a low or average standard. My outcome for this section is to provide you with the know-how to accomplish any task with perceived ease and excellence. By this I mean that any task, which is mentally and physically within your capability range, can be accomplished to a high standard of excellence if you know how to prepare yourself. The preparation not only creates the optimum state for doing the task, it also gives the perception of functional ease.

I said there were five reasons why tasks don't get done. These five reasons I have called strategies because they are just that – *avoidance strategies*. I shall begin by explaining strategies 1 and 2, then I will show you how to deal with them before moving on to strategy 3. When you arrive at the *sixth strategy*, which is an accomplishment

Before you do anything, you need to motivate yourself to *want* to do it.

Goals **that are not also *wants* are unlikely to be achieved.**

As a role model and example of how to be for your team, creating an image of self-mastery will have a positive influence.

strategy, you will know how to create a sixth strategy state for yourself any time you need it. The sixth strategy is any method you use for getting into a state of high self-motivation, and any number of NLP techniques may be used depending upon the avoidance strategy you want to overcome.

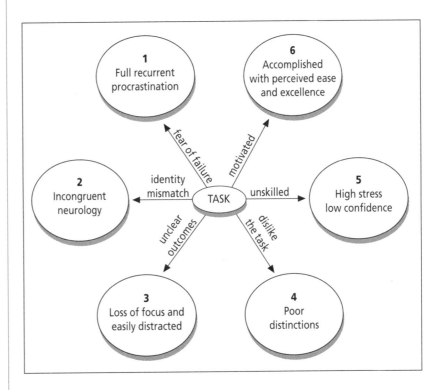

■ FIGURE 4.1
The sixth strategy

■ Fear of failure

This strategy is probably one of the major limitations to personal development. It is also one of the easiest to change, often resulting in instant and astounding results. This is usually a belief level limitation, i.e. *if I attempt this task I will probably fail and take a blow to my self-esteem and professional credibility*. Perception of status in the organization is also at stake here. The limitation is sometimes so strong that it can create full recurrent procrastination for particular tasks.

Avoidance strategies to deal with this can become very complex indeed. I know some people who plan their family holidays at specific times to avoid being confronted with the decision to be involved

The energy required to generate different excuses for not doing something can lead to stress.

in certain activities. The energy required to generate different excuses for not doing something can lead to stress. The journalist who interviewed me had a limiting belief about calling editors with scoops, and whenever she thought about it she created strong visual images of the different ways she could fail. Many sales people have limiting beliefs around cold calling and selling at director level in organizations.

Thinking about situations in which we have convinced ourselves that the outcome will be unpleasant for us burns-in failure to our neurology, and this is what we respond to. We create our own maps for failure and design avoidance strategies to deal with it. *What a waste of energy!*

Beliefs are very closely linked to identity. Exercise 1 (chapter 1) invited you to consider the labels you use around your identity. These labels form beliefs that act to reinforce who you are, so if you want to do something that you have never done before you must become someone who does that particular thing. Limiting beliefs act to preserve your current identity and stop you from changing because there is a certain comfort and security attached to who you are right now.

■ Identity mismatch

This strategy is saying *I am not the sort of person who does this thing*. It is an identity protector keeping you safely and securely locked into the thinking and behavior that is comfortable to you. When you become involved in a task which you have not identified as part of your role, you will generate signals of incongruence.

Quite often these signals will be caused by value conflicts. If the task you are doing has little value for you why are you doing it? If your results depend upon you completing this task why have you not attached a high enough value to it? You only exert energy and resources into activities that have value for you. Your identity labels describe you *as a person who values certain things*. My journalist acquaintance had not created the value and belief structure to change her identity into a person who sells scoops to editors.

If you take a few moments to think of the various tasks which involve you at work, and then attach a commitment indicator to each

We create our own maps for failure and design avoidance strategies to deal with it. *What a waste of energy!*

Limiting beliefs act to preserve your current identity and stop you from changing.

You only exert energy and resources into activities that have value for you.

"When you commit
with yourself fully,
the gods go with
you."

one, say on a scale of 1–10, how many would you score at ten? For those which may be less than ten, why are you not fully committed to the task? To fully commit yourself to anything requires an alignment of all the levels of learning and change – identity, values, beliefs, capabilities, behavior and environment. There is a saying which goes "when you commit with yourself fully, the gods go with you."

You may be thinking of tasks or activities that are important to you, where you want to modify your values and beliefs to create a slightly different you – a you that can confidently accomplish these tasks with perceived ease and excellence. Perhaps a high level meeting with a boss or a particular client. Perhaps a presentation to the company. A major project could be coming your way, or maybe you have been asked to manage a merger for the first time. Whatever the task ahead, if to accomplish it with ease and excellence you will require different behaviors and/or thought processes, the next exercise invites you to design a sixth strategy state of excellence. I'll run through the exercise using one of the examples above, leaving you to substitute your own particular situation as appropriate.

 **EXERCISE 5**

Sixth strategy state

For the purpose of this exercise I will assume the role of a business unit manager who has been asked to manage a major project for a prestigious new client. I have never managed a project of this size and importance before, in fact I have avoided large projects in the past because project management isn't something that I want to do, although I am aware that to take my department to more challenging heights in the organization I will have to take on a large project some time.

Depending upon the circumstances of the required change, I could use one of many NLP techniques and in this case a Swish (exercise 3, chapter 2) may be appropriate. The technique I will use in this scenario, however, is creating a new part, and I will use it to help me redefine my identity and belief systems around project management.

Step 1: What would it be like?

There is a part of me that has some objection to doing *project management*, and I must first discover, from within, precisely what this objection is. What stops me from plunging enthusiastically into the role of project management? What would have to change for this objecting part of me to be comfortable with project management? I begin to imagine myself as a project manager and fully associate into the role. This technique is called "future pacing" – constructing an experience as if it is happening now. So I imagine what it will be like performing the role of a project manager as I keep my internal senses alert for signals that explain the reason for the objection.

I begin to feel heavy in my stomach area and I feel a frown forming on my forehead. What is it that is making me feel uncomfortable about this? In my mind's eye I see myself at the end of the project. I am in a meeting with the project board and they are discussing the problems with the project. It's all my fault, I didn't manage it in a professional way (this is my internal dialog cutting in now). I wasn't trained to manage this level of resource and to own this level of responsibility. I failed to notice when things began to go wrong.

Step 2: Assessing the feedback

The feedback from this process tells me that I have issues around skills, responsibility, professionalism and noticing when things are going wrong. I now ask myself "would it be OK to manage a large project if (i) I were trained, (ii) I could handle the increased responsibility with ease, (iii) I would be perceived by the project board as a professional, and (iv) I could remain focussed on the work so that I would notice at an early stage when things were likely to go wrong?" I want a response from my objecting part here so I associate again with the role, this time adding these four resources, and check internally for signs of incongruence.

Step 3: Construct the new part

What will I look like when I am managing a large project with all these added resources? As I visualize this scenario in the future I stay alert to any signals of conflict. How does it feel now that I am becoming a professional project manager? I have read some books on project management, I have sought advice from some of our highly skilled project managers, I have booked myself onto a course to learn about managing projects and I am confident about keeping focussed and projecting a professional image of myself.

I run the movie through my mind of exactly what I will be doing to ensure my success as a project manager. The submodalities are intensifying now, brighter, more color, larger, three dimensional. I can hear what I am saying to the people around me, and what they are saying to me. I look and feel like a professional. I know how to be a project manager. I have a new part now that *is* a project manager. The part with the original objection no longer objects. I am a project manager.

Step 4: Check the ecology

So far the exercise has concentrated solely on you. It is important to also consider wider implications of a change of this nature, particularly with those around you – family, friends, colleagues, and any other significant people in your life. Check for signals of incongruence as you answer the question "how will this change affect these people and my relationship with them?" It may not be purposeful to become a superb project manager if by doing so it adversely affects other areas of your life.

This process is all about creating an identity for yourself that is congruent. You can do this in five to ten minutes, although it could take up to half an hour depending on how quickly you are able to identify the objections. I have used it many times to create parts I need to do new things. It does not take the place of gaining new skills. You still need to acquire those, but what it does do is to create the motivation for you to book the training and seek guidance from experts.

Once you have an identity as a project manager you'll be surprised at how easily the skill will come. Confidence and identity can develop through more conventional means, with skills training for example, but it takes much longer and often doesn't identify or deal with limiting beliefs or identity conflicts. The sixth strategy state gets you there quicker and in a more resourceful state of mind and body.

■ Unclear outcomes

Do you ever find it difficult to concentrate on the task in hand? An obvious cause for this is when there is something else playing on your mind – either a decision to make or a situation that is begging to be resolved and you haven't thought of a solution yet. Pick any day of the week and you will probably have a number of these unresolved problems or decisions zapping around your neurology.

Major problems such as serious illnesses or heavy duty financial problems are likely to distract you from most tasks, although even these situations can be controlled if necessary. I am more concerned here with thoughts that zap into your mind like "did I feed the cat this morning?" or, "who should I include for the memo about the new product launch tomorrow?" when you are trying to concentrate on a completely different task.

One cause for this lack of focus and ease of distraction is *unclear outcomes*. Sometimes it is possible to get so involved in detail that you deviate from the main purpose for what you are doing. Computer applications packages are great for stimulating this one. Have you ever found yourself putting a report or presentation together and suddenly found that you are doing the work of the publishing department instead? It can be great fun, but if it's not tied in to your outcomes it's not likely to get you anywhere.

There's an easy answer to this one. It was covered in chapter 3 – well formed outcomes. If ever you find yourself putting energy into something and being unclear about the outcome – stop! Check back with your outcomes and make whatever change is necessary to get back on track before you waste any more time. Motivation needs direction which is operationalized through outcomes. A lack of clarity in one's outcomes isn't the only cause of distraction and lack of focus but it is a common one. Dislike of the task is another.

If ever you find yourself putting energy into something and being unclear about the outcome – stop!

Motivation needs direction which is operationalized through outcomes.

■ Dislike of the task

Every now and then I get to cook dinner. I usually want to get it over with as quickly as possible so I can get on with some reading or other activity. Cooking has never been one of my favorite pursuits. Do you have tasks that are like this at work? I used to detest signing heaps of invoices to authorize payment for training courses, and reviewing supplier lists, which was such a tedious and uninteresting job. Regardless of my feelings about these tasks they were very important. If we didn't pay our suppliers they would withdraw their services, and if we didn't review the supplier list we could screw up the training schedule. If I don't cook the dinner we go hungry.

There needs to be some intrinsic value in the task for you to be fully motivated.

It's my guess that you can think of some tasks that you have similar feelings about. The problem is, that if you are not fully motivated to do something, and to be fully motivated there needs to be some perceived intrinsic value in the task for you, you will not make the distinctions you need to make in order to accomplish the task with perceived ease and excellence. When my wife cooks the dinner she makes fine distinctions about the ingredients because it is important to her. The type of distinction I make is whether or not I am burning the rice. My wife's distinctions are more about the right combinations of texture, flavour and seasoning.

There is no single reason why you may be either interested or disinterested in any particular task – this strategy tends to be much more deeply embedded into the neurology. You may be able to delegate some tasks which you prefer not to do, but as you make changes to your identity and values, and as you make smooth and swift transitions to new roles that present themselves, you will discover there are some tasks you would rather leave alone. The reason for this can be found in our metaprogram profile.

Metaprograms

Metaprograms are deletion filters (refer to figure 2.2, chapter 2). They directionalize our attention by deleting information and creating systematic, habitual patterns of thinking and behavior. Metaprograms may differ across contexts, and in organizations they can help to explain preferences for job types and provide insights as to why some people are able to excel at particular tasks that others struggle with. These systematic and habitual patterns are called metaprograms because they program our behavior at a level of influence that is over and above (meta) everything else.

I am going to introduce you to ten metaprograms that give clues as to how people are likely to respond in a given situation. They are explained below in stereotype form for learning purposes only. In reality you will find it misleading to label people as *this* or *that* type. They are useful only as an insight to behavioral patterns. One way of identifying someone's metaprogram patterns is by the words they choose, so I have provided some examples for you. You will also be reflecting on your own language and attempting to determine your own current metaprogram profile. This is highly recommended.

1 Motivational direction	*towards – away*
2 Activity content	*things – people*
3 Work pattern	*options – procedures*
4 Level of activity	*proactive – reactive*
5 Chunk size	*global – specifics*
6 Attention direction	*self – others*
7 Reference sort	*internal – external*
8 Group behavior	*task – maintenance*
9 Relationship filter	*match – mismatch*
10 Comparison sorts	*quantitative – qualitative*

■ TABLE 2
Metaprograms

Motivational direction (towards – away)   This was a feature of the well formed outcomes in chapter 3 – *positively stated*. People are either motivated towards or away from something or other. "Towards" people know what they want and create their own motivation to reach their outcomes. "Away from" people find it difficult to agree outcomes or objectives because they are more focussed on what to avoid. A towards person will talk about what they want. An away from person will talk about what they don't want. Away from people are suited to jobs where they can find problems, like quality departments, but don't ask them for solutions as they may never be able to decide which one to go for. Towards people are good at anything that requires a go-for-it mentality, which covers many jobs in modern organizations today.

Activity content (things – people)   This is important for companies in the service industry who need to project a sincere customer care attitude. People whose focus is on *things* are less aware of people's needs and may even be uncomfortable in conversation, particularly in complaint situations. They seem more interested in fixing the broken machine than in responding to the state of the customer. Being *people*-focussed is better for jobs at the customer interface as they are more sensitive and responsive to the customer's needs.

   In the computer industry we have found that it is easier to employ engineers who are people-focussed and teach them engineering skills than it is to employ good engineers who focus on technology, and teach them people skills. This latter situation is a struggle. People-focussed people will talk to you about who they were with and what was said while people who are oriented more towards things will omit this detail and tell you about materials, tools, technology, machines etc.

Work pattern (options – procedures)   These are very interesting patterns in business, and perhaps one of the easiest to identify through observing behavior. Some people prefer to have a well-written procedure to follow, and will create their own if one doesn't exist. However, they will create a procedure to reflect what actually happens – they are not very good at designing new procedures, you need an options person to do that.

Options people like to have variety and choice. They are excellent brainstormers and good all round ideas people, but they dislike being constrained by rigid procedures. They also like to keep their options open for as long as possible, so expect them to procrastinate over decisions. If you ask the question "Why did you choose your last holiday?," options people will give you reasons why they chose it such as "the price was right" or "we liked it last year." Procedures people will tell you *how* they chose their holiday "I went to the travel agents" etc. – they give you their procedure. Procedures people are ideal for jobs that have strict rules and processes. Options people prefer work that gives them plenty of variety and options.

Level of activity (proactive – reactive)   This is straightforward. Some people prefer to be proactive, others like being reactive. Reactive people are the fire-fighters. When the phone stops ringing they take a rest and wait for it to continue. Proactive people on the other hand will make use of time between calls to make improvements to the systems, and will enjoy jobs that offer scope to make changes and improve quality.

The type of jobs that suit reactive people are telephone help desks, receptionists, or anything that is based on a responsive service. Proactive people would suffer from stress in these occupations. Proactive people talk about what they are going to do, while reactive people talk about what they have done.

Chunk size (global – specifics)   Global people like to talk globally. They want to see the big picture and are less concerned about detail. If you were to ask a global person about a recent film they had seen you would get something like "it was a good thriller – better than the last one I saw." A detail person would keep your ears pinned back for hours telling you all the details of each character and each part of the story. Detail people tend to talk more sequentially while global people jump around across topics freely. Global people would become stressed in a job requiring lots of detailed analysis or description, and detail people would find it hard to cope in jobs demanding global thinking.

Attention direction (self – others)   This pattern is important in any industry where the focus must be on people 100 percent such as nursing or social work. It is also important in the training industry. People whose attention is directed outwards towards others make great nurses, social workers and trainers because of their genuine concern for the well being of others. It is as if they have antennae out constantly picking up signals of discomfort or deviation from some desired outcome.

People with attention focussed inwards, on self, are more concerned with how they are feeling or how they are progressing towards their outcomes. They often miss many of the signals of discomfort or deviation from other people. In my experience these people can be great motivational speakers, but lousy trainers.

Reference sort (internal – external)   This pattern is about feedback on standards. People with an internal reference instinctively know if they have done a good job. People with an external reference need someone else to tell them. Successful entrepreneurs are extremely internally referenced – they know when they have made a good or a bad decision. Many people in organizations are externally referenced and need a management structure to give them feedback on the standard of their work.

Group behavior (task – maintenance)   This is about the focus of energy in team situations. Some people have a strong association with task and this will be at the forefront of their thinking regardless of any team disputes or personal indifferences. Other people are more associated with team maintenance functions and will seem to have less of a regard for the task in hand when there are problems within the team. Task-oriented people perform well in jobs where they can get their head down without having to deal with too many other people. Maintenance-oriented people need jobs where it is important to establish and maintain good relationships such as public relations or customer service.

Relationship filter (sameness – difference)   There are four main orientations which determine how people sort information from their environment to learn and understand.

● *Similarity*   Some people display a tendency to look for "what's there" as opposed to "what's missing." There is a focus on commonality, and how things fit together. There is a danger for people with a strong similarity sort to generalize very quickly, and to form assumptions. They also have difficulty coping with organizational change, and prefer long-term steady employment. They may stay in the same job happily for 20–25 years.

● *Similarity with exceptions*   This filter looks for similarity first, with a secondary emphasis on difference. During conversations you can tell when someone is using this filter by their use of comparatives such as *more, better, less, except, but, although*. People who evaluate relationships using this filter don't mind change as long as it is gradual and not too frequent. They will typically remain in the same job for 5–7 years before looking for something different.

● *Difference*   This filter can be pedantically detailed and tedious. A strong orientation to difference will cause a person to perpetually see how things don't work, or don't fit together. They will look for difference in everything, sorting for "what's missing." They tend to become restless in a job after 9–18 months.

● *Difference with exceptions*   This filter focusses first on "what's different" with a secondary emphasis on "what's the same." When someone is using this relationship filter they will typically say "It's a refreshing change, although the hours are the same." People using this filter will tend to stay in a job for 18–36 months.

Comparison sorts (qualitative – quantitative)   Comparison sorts are filters for selecting information with which to make a decision. The information can be either qualitative or quantitative. This is simply a "more/less than" sort or a "better/worse than" sort. People have different preferences for each one and will generally make decisions based on their particular filter. Some managers make decisions based solely upon the amount of money to be made, or costs to be reduced, and give little regard to qualitative consequences. The reverse of this is also prevalent.

These ten metaprograms are a selection of the ones you will find most useful in organizational life. Once you are able to identify them you will notice the effect they have on how differently people approach their jobs.[1] This has a significant influence on their results. You may already be applying these to explain puzzling behavior of people you know at work, and in later chapters we will be using them to do just that.

However, the purpose of introducing you to metaprograms in this section is to give you an insight into your own thinking and behavior. Are there some tasks that you would rather not do? Can you identify where a metaprogram may explain this situation?

One of the questions I am often asked is "can you change your metaprogram profile?" The answer is yes, and it takes time. There may be reasons why you want to adopt an alien metaprogram for long-term gains, or alternatively you may wish to adopt one to help you use a particular strategy for a short-term gain. The best process to use for this is to model someone who has the metaprogram you want, and who uses it to achieve what you also want to achieve.

Modeling

NLP is a modeling technology, and it is highly effective for modeling other people's generalizations, distortions and deletions. It is not possible to cover modeling in its entirety – I could fill a whole book

[1] For a free information pack on the influence of metaprograms, and a metaprogram questionnaire, contact Paragon.

[2] For a free information pack on "perforamnce modeling," contact Paragon.

on the subject of behavioral modeling.[2] However, I can provide you with some basics, and as we all adopt behaviors from our role models unconsciously anyway, the following information will start you thinking about doing it with purpose and intention.

My personal profile used to include an *external reference* sort. In modeling the people I most wanted to be like, and in setting my long-term outcomes, I realized that I would have to change this metaprogram. I constructed pictures in my mind of how I wanted to be with these changes on board. I began to observe and model the behavior generated from these metaprograms by my role models. I am a very kinesthetic person so I would take a few minutes after completing a task to say to myself "how do I feel about this?" . . . "how do I know I am satisfied with my work?" . . . "there is no point in asking anyone else about my work because I know the standard I have achieved" . . . "and I know because I can feel that I know".

Sometimes I catch myself reverting back to my old pattern of needing external feedback – I have lived with that pattern for a long time, but I can deal with the odd regression quite easily now.

If you are a strong *global* person, you may find it useful on occasion to make fine distinctions within a detailed document, the sort of distinctions that you would expect from a *specifics* person. Perhaps it's a financial spreadsheet or a legal document. Who do you know with the best strategy for picking the bones out of this type of document? Find this person and model them. Observe their physiology as they are performing the task, particularly the following aspects:

- **Breathing** – rhythm, speed, depth, chest or stomach area.
- **Posture** – leaning forward/back, left/right, head position, shoulders.
- **Voice** – Pitch, tonality, resonance, speed, rhythm.

These are the main elements of physiology to model. What you are doing is being like them, and you know that the mind and body are one system and that they affect each other, so by taking on their physiology it will be easier to think like them.

In addition to modeling physiology you may want to take on the person's value and belief system also, but make sure that it is ecological with the rest of your environment first. You wouldn't want to adopt the value system of a megalomaniac, for example. Select your modeling subjects with care!

■ Unskilled

Returning now to the sixth strategy model, another reason for not completing a task is that you may be missing the skills required. Persisting with a task, unskilled, often leads to stress and in some cases low levels of confidence. Some organizations are very good at giving people tasks without providing the skills to go with it.

Becoming a manager is typical of this situation. It is such a vast area to understand, and there are so many learning materials available it is often difficult to know what you should be studying. Some organizations like to think that they have this pinned down with clear development programs designed to deliver a set of management competencies. Turning this type of learning into management accomplishment of practical everyday tasks however takes a long time. How many days does a manager expect to invest in learning how to manage resources in an organization? If you take the conventional route you never stop counting. I could open my office mail any day of the week and find details of management training that add up to over 100 days (not including MBAs etc). The list would include different short courses from giving presentations to problem solving in groups.

The point I am making is not that conventional training should be scrapped, quite the contrary. It's the mindset and expectation that goes with this type of skills acquisition that I object to because it reinforces an environment where learning equals classroom, and so if you are not in the classroom you are not learning. Most (if not all) management courses are about communicating. Organizations need to understand how learning occurs and really begin to harness feedback.

I highly recommend Peter Senge's[3] work on learning organizations which provides some excellent examples of what organizations could do to begin fostering learning environments. NLP is all about human communication, learning and change. As a manager, you can decide to have a learning environment in your part of the organization. We can learn a great deal from each other.

Select your modeling subjects with care!

Some organizations are very good at giving people tasks without providing the skills to go with it.

Organizations need to understand how learning occurs and really begin to harness feedback.

[3] Peter Senge, *The Vth Discipline*, Doubleday; 1990.

■ Motivated – the *sixth strategy state!*

Let me tell you more about my friend, the journalist. I was intrigued to discover how many hidden talents she had which helped her to achieve her current success. I asked her what her strategy was for finding a story and writing it up, to which she replied:

> "I look for all the places where I might find information, choose the most interesting place to be, go there, get my story and write it up. I never miss an editorial deadline. Even if it's the night before the deadline I know I will get the story in, even if I have to stay up all night writing."

The voice tonality and whole physiology was completely congruent with the message. This is clearly a winning strategy fueled with high octane self-motivation. It is also a visual strategy " . . . I *look* for places . . ." So, my next question was "what would happen if you were to use this strategy for calling new editors with your scoops? Can you see a similarly desired and conclusive result?"

We all have a range of strategies for doing all kinds of things. Some strategies are more useful than others. Our strategies are made up of neurological responses to situations, that is they contain both mind and body patterns. We have strategies that we use to motivate ourselves which I have called *sixth strategy states*. Top performance requires high states of motivation. We can move strategies between contexts, so that if we are getting great results in one activity we can use the same *sixth strategy state* to improve our performance in another area.

Whenever you catch yourself running an avoidance strategy you now have the know-how to choose differently. If the task you are avoiding is something that will move you towards your outcomes, a sixth strategy state will get you there.

I will leave you to think about this, and about some of the tasks which you would prefer to accomplish with perceived ease and excellence. Take an inventory of the following and choose where a change might have the desired effect. It could be a belief. It could be an identity level change. It could be more rooted than that in your metaprogram profile. It could be a value conflict, or perhaps it is simply a skill deficit. Do you know someone who does this skill ele-

Strategies are made up of neurological responses to situations, that is they contain both mind and body patterns.

Top performance requires high states of motivation.

gantly? Do you have a state of high self-motivation for another task than can be easily transferred to this task?

Here's a table which you can use to record these and other important dimensions of self for individual tasks. You may find it interesting, and useful, to interview a model of excellence for a task you want to improve at, and record their profile on a sixth strategy table.

In other living creatures the ignorance of themselves is nature, but in men it is a vice.
Boethius (480–525)
Roman philosopher

■ **TABLE 3**
Sixth strategy profile table

Task description	

Outcomes	
Positively stated	
Resourced	
Initiated and maintained by self	
Ecological	
Sensory based evidence criteria	
Time phased	

Identity labels	
Values	
Beliefs	
Capabilities	
Behavior	
Environment	

Metaprograms	
toward/away	
things/people	
options/procedures	
proactive/reactive	
global/specific	
self/others	
int./ext. reference	
task/maintenance	
relationship	
comparison	

LEADERSHIP

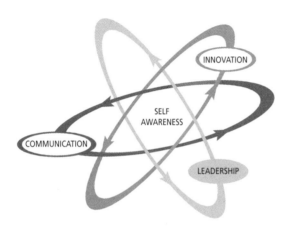

INNOVATION

SELF
AWARENESS

COMMUNICATION

LEADERSHIP

TIME

*It is a nice reflection
that the clock as we
know it, the pacemaker
strapped to our pulse or
the pocket dictator of
modern life, had since
the Middle Ages fired
the skill of craftsmen
too, in a leisurely way.
In those days the early
clock-makers wanted,
not to know the time of
day, but to reproduce
the motions of the
starry heavens.*

DR JACOB BRONOWSKI,
The Ascent of Man,
British scientist

**Time is a concept
that exists for us as
motion, and so we
use motion to
conceptualize
time into our
experience.**

Modern metaphors for time

From Aristotle to Einstein, a host of scientists and philosophers throughout the ages have explored the concept of time. The seasonal cycle is nature's clock telling us when to plant seed and when to reap the harvest. Time is a concept that exists for us as motion, and so we use motion to conceptualize time into our experience. Man's early attempts at building clock-like mechanisms were designed to reproduce the movement of the planets, unlike today's computerized clocks designed with integrated diaries and personal organizers that help us manage our lives, and squeeze as much as possible into our existence.

I have often heard the culture of modern business life referred to as a QFN – *quicker, faster, now,* culture. Technology companies are particularly focussed on getting new innovations to the market before anyone else. Product life-cycles are becoming shorter and the speed of innovation gets quicker. Modern marketing methods typify the QFN culture, and I wonder just how fast each end of the *product development/life-cycle* continuum are coming together.

This is not a pessimistic reflection, rather one of curiosity. At the moment we play the QFN game because our perceived quality of life depends upon us being in the game. At some point in the future, the dynamics of the continuum will change in such a way that a new game will emerge with a different set of dynamics. This new game will present a step change in the way organizations operate, and within it "time" will be one constant that determines its new form and function. Whatever the future of organizational life, leaders in business today need the ability to manage themselves and their business *in* and *through* time, while having an awareness of how the dynamics of business may change in relation to time.

The main ideas offered in this chapter build on the concepts developed in section one, and further strengthen the learning process in the generative management development model (figure 1, Introduction) with the inclusion of time into the feedback process. Results in the area of Leadership depend upon having an appropriate awareness of time with the flexibility to change how you code time should your current timeline be hindering progress.

The way you code time acts as a perceptual filter to form your own unique experience of the world. Turning ideas into action is as much about *when* you do something as *what* you do and *how* you do it. In your directional role as conductor, the orchestra is relying upon you to keep the time so that everyone knows precisely when to play their part. As a leader who uses feedback to develop personal mastery, you must be the master of time and not allow time to be the master of you or your destiny.

Analyzing the language we use about time gives clues about the way we allow time to act upon our experience metaphorically. If you listen to the different metaphors implied when people talk about time you can begin to understand some of the limitations we create for ourselves. Here are some common idioms with their metaphorical presuppositions:

- *I haven't got time for that* (time is a possession – something you have or haven't got)

- *I can't make the time to do that* (time can be manufactured)

- *There's never enough time* (time is a commodity which is always in short supply)

- *Time is against us* (time has physical form and energy)

- *Time is on our side* (time can choose to take sides)

- *We have all the time in the world* (time is contained by the world and we can own it)

- *Time waits for no-one* (time is inconsiderate)

These are all metaphors which we use every day to express our relationship with time. It may seem quite harmless to say these things, but it does have an effect on our behavior. The metaphorical language we use is a perceptual filter on time and therefore influences how we code time (our timeline). The way we interpret time through our metaphors can dictate how we operate in our environment.

As a leader who uses feedback to develop personal mastery, you must be the master of time and not allow time to be the master of you or your destiny.

The way we interpret time through our metaphors can dictate how we operate in our environment.

Time as an investment portfolio

One of the strongest metaphors used today is that of time as units of currency. We *spend* time and we *invest* time. We can choose to invest these units of currency where we please and take risks on the return. This is a useful metaphor if you invest *some* time in deciding where to invest the *rest*. Taking time out to plan on a regular basis will have the highest return of all, and will minimize any risk. If you invest your time unwisely you will get feedback to help you decide where best to invest the next 24 hours allocated to you. The return on your investment can be thought of as the results you get for yourself, your team and your organization.

Modern methods of time management include family and social dimensions to time investment, both of which are high priority areas, and I encourage you to focus on these areas also. As this is a business

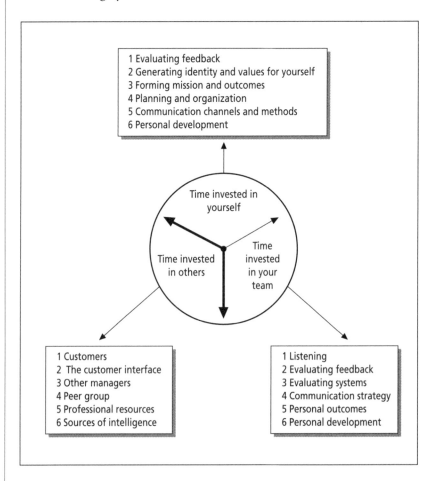

■ FIGURE 5.1
The time investment portfolio

book about business management, I will concentrate on investment purely in the business context. Figure 5.1 shows an ideal time investment portfolio for delivering high gain and low risk.

Before describing each of the items in the portfolio it is worth listing the benefits of investing your time in this way.

■ Gains

Investing time in the way suggested by this portfolio will return high gains in commitment, respect, productivity, quality of work output and loyalty. In addition to these business gains there will be personal gains in self-esteem, learning, knowledge, confidence, and belonging for both team and leader.

■ Risks

The usual risks managers fear such as low motivation, poor communication, low customer satisfaction, complaints, errors, mistakes, poor judgments and general inefficiencies will be reduced to a minimum. In fact, because of the way you treat problems of this nature – as *feedback*, they all contribute to learning and development anyway – so you can't lose! There is no failure – only feedback.

NLP

There is no failure – only feedback.

■ Time invested in yourself

1 Evaluating feedback

This is possibly the highest priority you can put on time. Many managers seem to wander through organizational life responding to needs as they arise, only taking time to plan the obvious such as new projects, holidays, training courses etc. Spend some time out of every day in reflection of what happened the day before. Evaluate feedback and incorporate learning into the now and the future. It's not enough to let your autopilot do this for you as you drive home. Take some quality time and evaluate your feedback – use the feedback to generate new learning, development and progress.

2 Generating identity and values for yourself

Are your values still appropriate for the challenges before you? Can you identify with the tasks that must be accomplished to achieve

Are the activities that you attach importance to still of value to you and useful for achieving your outcomes?

your outcomes? Are there tasks before you that require knowledge and skills you have not yet fully acquired? Are the activities that you attach importance to still of value to you and useful for achieving your outcomes?

A manager responsible for quality in a timber company put a high value on employees using a specific set of problem-solving tools, and consequently spent a great deal of time communicating this message through expensive color-printed quality packs for all employees. The manager was so fixated on maintaining his quality policy that he ignored feedback from business managers saying that the tools were too complex and the quality messages too rigid and authoritarian. The values that were considered necessary for the success of the quality program during its implementation phase were no longer valid as managers became educated in quality systems. Also, the quality manager's identity was as an implementer of systems.

As the program grew in size and spread to more parts of the company he did not recognize the need to identify with employees as his customers. The manager was seen to be at fault, he was moved sideways and an external consultancy was taken on to rescue the program. Be aware that the values you put on the work of your department and the identity you have with your roles will change over time.

Be aware that the values you put on the work of your department and the identity you have with your roles will change over time.

3 Forming mission and outcomes

All organizations undergo change. They may grow, shrink, diversify, restructure, downsize, regroup, merge, demerge, centralize, decentralize, change markets, change CEOs, drop product lines, develop product lines, introduce policies, drop policies, change distribution methods, go international, refinance, delayer, divisionalize, go public . . . the list could probably fill the rest of the book. The point is that organizations change – they evolve – the static organization doesn't exist. So your department's mission and outcomes must evolve also, to maintain alignment with the global positioning of the organization. Review your outcomes against the global direction regularly – at least quarterly.

Review your outcomes against the global direction regularly – at least quarterly.

4 Planning and organization

Thinking systemically about your role in the global picture, how does the organization of your department contribute to these higher level outcomes? Are the inputs to your department appropriate for the processes, and are the outputs you are generating what your customers need? Reviewing your processes against feedback should be a constant ongoing activity involving all members of your team. Time invested in evaluating your work system and planning for future alignment will have big payoffs. This is where you can be seen as proactive, forward thinking and decisive by the people around you. The changes you make in this area will have the biggest effect on people, products and systems, so it is worth investing enough quality time to make sure you get it right.

5 Communication channels and methods

This is the commonest cause of problems in business, and its impact on organizational health cannot be understated. The name of the game in the late 1970s and early 1980s was productivity per employee. Today, organizations are desperate to improve methods of sharing information to gain competitive advantage. We are in the information age and communication is on everyone's agenda. A continual assessment of your communication channels and methods is a necessity. And even with the modern technology we have for communicating electronically, business is still very much about transactions between people.

Even with the modern technology we have for communicating electronically, business is still very much about transactions between people.

As people migrate across companies and roles, and new faces appear, weak links will develop in your communication lines – links that need re-forging to strengthen the web you have across the organization. Time spent in evaluating, constructing and strengthening your web of communication will pay huge dividends. When it comes to communication, an organization with a mission is much like an army. The most devastation is caused by cutting the lines of communication. What would happen to your business outcomes if you were suddenly cut off from all communication with colleagues, suppliers and customers? In section three I will be exploring communication strategy and process in greater detail.

6 Personal development

You have probably heard of the concept "the learning organization," which I wholeheartedly subscribe to and endorse as an ideal for organizations to aim for. If you have not come across this, I encourage you to take a look at the ideas it promotes. In reality of course, organizations don't learn, the people in them do. This is one reason why your own personal development is so crucial – your working environment is dependent upon your learning.

In addition to this, learning promotes health and longevity.[1] Recent brain research shows that once a brain is no longer stimulated by variety of experience (stops learning), senility begins to set in. Proactive, conscious and purposeful personal development planning is the answer here. Leaving your learning to unconscious evaluation of experience is not an effective way to learn. Spend some time deciding your next organized learning opportunity.

On all of the above areas, I recommend a minimum investment of 30 minutes per day, preferably at the start of each day, and at least three hours at the beginning of each month. This will of course differ from person to person depending upon your span of responsibility. Generally speaking, the wider the span, the more time you will need for reflection, evaluation and decision making on these items.

■ Time invested in your team

1 Listening

There should never be a time when you are not listening. The time invested in listening does not have to be time-scheduled in your diary, it is any time a member of your team is communicating with you. If you want your people to respect and believe in you, if you want them to follow your example, if you want them to be confident in their work – listen to them, take an interest in what they do and say, and show that you care about them and the problems they are dealing with. And listen to *understand*, not to reply. Most people, when they have a problem, just want someone to understand their situation – it's as if having someone in authority understand what they are struggling with enables them to deal with it.

There will, of course, be times when you will have to intervene and offer the benefit of your knowledge or experience, but interventions of this nature should be minimal. Be aware of when you need to listen. If you are busy working to a deadline on a report and one

[1] Eric Jensen, *The learning brain* Turning Point Publishing; 1994.

Spend some time deciding your next organized learning opportunity.

Listen to *understand*, not to reply.

of your people interrupts with a question, this is a time to listen, to give them your full attention regardless of the work you may be doing. If you can master this you have mastered the art of listening. This topic will be continued and expanded in the next chapter – Empowerment.

2 Evaluating feedback

This should be the topic of a regular department meeting. Brief all your people to capture feedback and bring it to the meeting for evaluation. The more open you are with this, the better will be the quality of the feedback you get. Avoid putting restrictions on feedback by categorizing, otherwise you will only get that which fits your map of what feedback should be about, and you will delete the rest.

3 Evaluating systems

This is an evaluation of the appropriateness of your working systems against your outcomes. Allow the team to do the work on this. Your role is to direct and orchestrate proceedings, not take control of the evaluation. You may provide frameworks or evaluation processes and contribute ideas, but the evaluation should be left to the people working the system. If you take control you also take ownership.

Aim to have one of these meetings at least every two months and combine it with the feedback evaluation if you want, but keep the two items separate otherwise you may dilute the value of feedback. Engender an informal environment, and make the meetings enjoyable while recording all decisions and actions against each participant. Make sure all meetings with your team are relevant and productive.

4 Communication strategy

What is your communication strategy, with your customers, your suppliers and others in the organization that would benefit from an awareness of your activities? This is about being proactive and having a communication strategy constructed around an intended outcome, rather than just allowing it to evolve out of the needs of your team.

A communication strategy should include methods of eliciting and capturing feedback, words and images presenting your team in a favorable light, useful information for others – as a minimum. The

We rarely develop true understanding relationships with voices over the phone or with e-mail messages.

strategy should also allow for developing relationships across your web of communication on a continual basis. Think of it as a spider that is always working to renew parts of the web that become damaged. This is best done on a face-to-face meeting basis since we rarely develop true understanding relationships with voices over the phone or with e-mail messages.

In organizations we must meet people face-to-face in order to have a quality relationship with them. If ever you have communication problems between two functions, the best way of resolving them is to bring the operators of each function together so that they can begin to understand and empathize with each other's environmental conditions. These concepts are further explored in section three – Communication.

5 Personal outcomes

This is simply a matter of being aware that individuals in your team have personal outcomes, and knowing what they are. These outcomes may or may not be work-related, but they will be important to the individual – they will have value for them. If you can help them achieve these values you will have been of service and strengthened the relationship between them, work and you – all the areas covered under high gain in the portfolio. One of my consultants is a superb theatrical performer and singer. I doubt that we would have such an understanding and productive relationship were I the type to allow this personal value to go unnoticed. The dynamic at work is one of understanding, listening, valuing and supporting.

There is one caveat to this advice, where the outcome is shrouded in negative emotions – perhaps an employee who is reluctant to travel on business because the partner becomes jealous. You may feel that counseling is the best approach, and you could be right, but be aware that sometimes people prefer to suffer the pain of their problems than expose them to others. If the issue is not affecting work performance it may be better to observe from a distance.

6 Personal development

Time invested in identifying training needs and development planning will ensure that your team members continue to learn new

The dynamic at work is one of understanding, listening, valuing and supporting.

things and their skills keep pace with new tasks that need to be accomplished. Feedback about how well tasks have been completed, and from department meetings where new processes may have been identified, will be useful here. Aim to keep a matrix of planned development events, including formal courses, for all your team members. Let them know each other's plans. Foster a "learning community" environment by the words you use and the emphasis you put on evaluating feedback, learning from experiences, making new discoveries and attending organized learning events.

■ Time invested in others

1 Customers

This is an obvious and common-sense area for investing your time. In fact the danger here is that possibly too much time can be spent with customers to the detriment of other areas in the portfolio. A balance is required. This is potentially a huge area and I shall not attempt to fulfill the requirements of a marketing strategy here, merely emphasize the importance of being with your customers on a frequent basis and listening to them – gathering feedback for purposes of marketing and customer satisfaction. This should be the case whether your customers are external to the organization or internal.

2 The customer interface

Being at the customer interface is different from being with your customers. This is being at the interaction between your team and your customers. The Japanese call this "walking the job," or it is more often referred to as "managing by walking about." If you refer back to the perceptual positions exercise (chapter 3, exercise 4), it's taking an observer, or meta position to customer and employee. It's noticing the interactions and getting feedback about the appropriateness of the transactions and of their consequences. You will get valuable information to indicate how well you are achieving your outcomes, or whether your outcomes are appropriate. You will also gain detailed insights into how your system and the customer's system influence each other, and many other details that constitute feedback.

3 Other managers and your peer group

Effective leaders keep their ears to the ground, their noses in the air, their feelers out and their eyes peeled for all and everything that is going on around them. Information about changes in one part of the organization will have an effect on your team in some way – we have learned this from systems theory. Don't wait to be taken by surprise, and don't allow rumoring to infiltrate your team. Do stay in the know and pre-empt any changes that are likely to affect your own team.

4 Professional resources and sources of intelligence

The business world is rife with new concepts, ideas and methodologies about how different functions should be reorganized to cope better with the complexities of organizational life. In the area of personal development you have a myriad of ideas from competencies, learning sets, key development areas, self-managed learning, computer-based learning, multi-media learning, simulations, the learning organization concept and a host of other ideas. In business processing you have the quality movement, re-engineering, procedures, Kaizen, JIT, the virtual organization and many other flavors from around the globe.

What do you take notice of with so much information out there? One of the things you need to know is that all new ideas are based on the concept of improvement, and improvement is generated out of learning from our own experience and the experiences of others. Make a point of joining professional institutes that provide information about ideas both old and new. Read professional magazines, like the *Harvard Business Review,* which is probably the best around today, although there are many other special interest magazines about. With so much material available you need to be selective and choose the material that is going to give you an all-round, balanced view of current thinking on business, organizational development, and your particular professional discipline.

Investing time is one decision you must get right, which is why I have dedicated a whole chapter (at least) to this subject. I also encourage you to read more on the subject of time, and continually appraise your investment portfolio. I will now expand more on the NLP metaphors of *in time* and *through time.*

■ Time modes

Albert Einstein was the first to join time to space. He presented to the world "the theory of relativity," that what we see is relative to what others see, that is – relative to our place and speed. Einstein was very much aware that each person experiences a different view of the world. In NLP we use space in a metaphorical way, and it seems natural that when we think of time we are able to attach a spatial aspect to it, otherwise we become stuck with the "pacemakers strapped to our pulse" which is not a very useful planning tool.

Diaries, planners and organizers are all methods of relating to time through space – *where* you put your diary entry is important. In NLP we use the metaphors of in time and through time, and at the end of this chapter you will be invited to work through a planning activity using a spatial timeline. The concept of "timeline" was introduced in chapter 2, and it is useful to make the distinction between the two modes and recognize that you have a choice.

There are times when you will want to be having an in-time experience such as at a party, or a business meeting with colleagues, for example. At other times it may be better to have a through-time experience, being an observer of what is going on around you. An acquaintance of mine is very good at being through-time during tough negotiations (this is her job). She can spend hours in a meeting listening in through-time mode while processing the dynamics of the negotiation in her mind using visuals and internal dialog. She changes her mode to in-time only when she has decided to make a contribution. She is an excellent negotiator.

People who are predominantly in-time are often late for appointments and poor planners. They prefer to be in the here and now. People who are predominantly through-time spend much of their existence as an observer of life rather than being part of what is going on around them. They make great planners, are usually prompt for their appointments, but often give the impression that although their body is with you their mind is elsewhere.

The ability to change modes according to the feedback you are getting is natural to some people and an acquired skill for others. I encourage you to notice, while investing time in each of the areas in your portfolio, whether you are in-time or through-time. You may wish to experiment with this and notice the results you get. Imagining a timeline where you can attach future events is a skill worth developing. Many people do this as a natural process.

From one of my management students I learned a wonderful process for knowing the date without the use of a calendar. I was amazed at how she could come up with any date on the current year's calendar. I discovered that she imagined the year as a "C" curve just to the right about two feet in front of her face. On this curve she plotted points for month ends with significant dates like the milestones of major projects "burned-in" at appropriate points. When she thought about a particular month, she would zoom in on that part of the curve and the numbers of each day would appear. We tested this in the training room and took time out for the other students to install the process because it was so effective.

Imagining time as a virtual spatial entity is worth experimenting with, and the next exercise offers you an opportunity to explore time as an actual spatial entity within the context of a planning activity.

EXERCISE 6

Planning for success

Is there a task coming up in the future that is important to you, your team or your organization, and at which you want to personally excel? Perhaps an important meeting, a planning session with your team, a customer presentation, a strategic report you have to write, a full blown multi-million dollar project, or a job interview? You are going to use a spatial metaphor to help build a successful event, so you will need plenty of physical space for this exercise.

Step 1

[2] Tad James, *Timeline therapy and the basis of personality* Meta Publications; 1988.

Imagine that your future[2] timeline projects out in front of you onto the floor – as if you are rolling out a red carpet.

Step 2

Place an image of you succeeding in this future task on the timeline at a distance that feels right to you. Make the image a bright colorful one – use the critical submodalities you identified with the Swish technique to intensify it. The image can be on any plane, it can be 3D, moving, and with sound effects if you like.

Step 3

Now walk down your timeline, stop when you are on top of your image and become fully associated with the feeling of success in this task. Can you feel how good it is to be that successful? You can enjoy this feeling for a few moments.

Step 4

Continue walking now, just past your image. Stop and turn around so that you are looking down your timeline back to the *now* point. You should be focussing on the time between *now* and your image of success (refer to figure 5.2). As you focus your thinking on this time span, imagine all the things you had to do to ensure your success. Here are some examples of useful questions to focus your thinking:

- What feedback did you get the last time you performed this operation?
- What plans did you have to make?
- Who had to be informed about your task?
- Who did you need to communicate with?
- What method of communication was most relevant?
- Did you need extra skills – and how did you acquire them?
- Was advice from experienced and successful people helpful to you?
- Did you need time to rehearse and/or practice?

What you are doing at this stage is visualizing having done all the things you need to do in order to achieve a successful task. When you are comfortable that everything has been considered you can begin to fit them onto your timeline in the places that seem most appropriate.

Step 5

When you have all your images in place on your timeline you are ready to walk back to the original now position where you started from, pausing momentarily over each image to fully associate into the activity. When you arrive back at your original position and look down your timeline, are you confident that each of the tasks you have identified is sufficiently detailed to ensure your success? If the answer is yes, you have completed the exercise. If you have any doubt or uncertainty then take another walk down your timeline until you get to the place where the doubt is generated and make whatever adjustments you consider are necessary.

This process will give you feedback about the reality of your planned time allocation for completing the task. Have you invested sufficient time in all the necessary areas in order to ensure you achieve your outcome, without a question of doubt? The questions above are provided as examples only and are certainly not exhaustive. You may find your own questions more relevant to your particular chosen task.

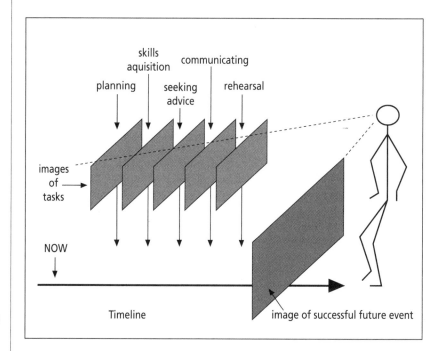

■ **FIGURE 5.2**
Building success into future events

This technique is very popular with many of my management students. It can be used to build success into any future task, although it is particularly useful for major events and where you have little experience to draw upon. It has many advantages over conventional diary entry planning which tends to be done very hurriedly and in a fully dissociated state. How often do you find yourself committed to someone else's project plan where the timescale for completion has been set before you have had the chance to consider what you need to do? This situation prevails in many customer-focussed organizations – you rarely seem to have time to do a "proper job" where someone else has overall authority for the project.

The result of this is to cut planning time which is often unrecognized as a productive activity. Timeline planning, particularly for important projects, is very thorough and effective. Used in conjunction with other NLP techniques it enables you to build in robustness, certainty and accomplishment into your futures.

Time goes, you say? Ah, no!

Alas, Time stays; we go.

Austin Dobson
(1840–1921),
British author

EMPOWERMENT

- **Defining empowerment**

- **The difference empowerment makes**

- **Power**

- **Conditions for producing generative power**

- **Two important first lessons about empowerment**

- **A question of respect**

- **Pacing and leading**

- **Reframing**

- **The empowering leader**

The authoritarian culture *– coercive power*/ The technical culture *– expert power* / The learning culture *– generative power* / Lesson number one *– the easy solution* / Lesson number two *– my people don't want to be empowered* / WIIFM *– or what's in it for me?* / The leader as teacher / The leader as coaching enabler

The purpose of getting power is to be able to give it away.
ANEURIN BEVAN
(1897–1960)
British Labour politician

Empowerment is a condition determined by a policy. For many people the verb "to empower" is normally associated with government. The police force are empowered to keep law and order by means of a government policy and a set of guidelines, or rules, governing their behavior – what they *are* and *are not* allowed to do. The policies and guidelines refer to the decisions they are allowed to make such as when to use force, when to take into custody or decisions on the length of time a suspect can be detained etc. The government is a higher order whose role includes empowering others to make *some*, but not *all* decisions.

In organizational life empowerment has, in recent years, risen to a high position on the human resource director's agenda as a result of the stripping out of layers of middle management decision makers. Someone has to make the decisions, so it will have to rest with the people actually doing the work. But they won't be allowed to decide everything – some things are not negotiable such as wage levels and structure, markets, headcount, investment etc. Looking for answers to the question "how much empowerment?" will lead you to the problems many organizations and individual managers struggle with when they attempt to introduce it.

This chapter is concerned more with the *how* of empowerment than the *what*. There are many books on the management bookshelf advising you on *what* to do to bring about empowerment. Here I will provide you with a model of the conditions of empowerment from which to work with the *how*.

First, there is a more fundamental *why* question to answer. After all you may already be an empowering leader to a greater or lesser degree, or you may want to know more about the subject before you can convince yourself that it is worth the effort. Whatever motivation your experience and curiosity creates, it will be influenced by your values, and it will also be connected in some way to your identity and your beliefs. I invite you to think now about your own perceptions of *you the leader*, as you discover more about the type of leader you want to become.

Defining empowerment

The following definition of empowerment seems to be the most appropriate for the modern organization.

- *Empowerment is a business methodology giving employees responsibility and authority for decisions at the level at which they operate.*
- *Empowerment challenges the traditional role of the manager as a decision maker/problem solver and redefines the role as an enabler/coach.*

Empowerment is based around the concept that problems are best solved by the people working with the problem, and not by some higher order of management. This argument makes sense since the higher up the organization you get, the less you will know about operational problems. Total Quality Management initiatives are based upon this concept.

Empowerment is a business methodology which challenges the traditional role of the manager.

The difference empowerment makes

Organizational environments that empower people put fewer limitations and boundaries on structure. They nurture and reinforce learning cultures where change, skills, achievement and progress are high values, and rules and procedures are lower ones. They put more emphasis on contribution than status, and they reward achievement not responsibility – this results from a sincere belief that success is achieved through people.

The empowered organization stimulates creativity and "off-the-wall" individuality bringing greater variety into people's working day. It thrives on complexity and ambiguity, having the flexibility to respond in many different ways to changes in market environments. It treats problems as opportunities and isn't afraid of owning up to mistakes. A truly empowered organization is the organization of progress, achievement, and focus on the future.

In contrast to this, organizations that do not empower people often value status and position or knowledge and expertise over actual contribution. Procedure and protocol are more important

A truly empowered organization is the organization of progress, achievement, and focus on the future.

than finding innovative solutions. Working norms are highly respected, and there are usually recognized ways of getting things done. Problems cause embarassment and often get swept under the carpet only to re-emerge at a later date. The disempowered organization is the organization of sameness, procedure, rules, protocol and focus on today.

Power

The definition of power is *"the rate at which a body or system does work."* Think about an engine, with the output rated in horsepower. Gasoline and air combust in the engine to produce horsepower. So power is *produced* from an interaction between the fuel and the engine. The engine converts the power of the combusion to movement through its transmission system. If you listen to mechanics talking about engines you will hear them use words like performance and behavior: *"the engine behaves really well on unleaded gasoline."* And any mechanic will tell you how important the mix of gasoline and air is to the performance of the engine.

This is an apt metaphor for the way organizations produce power to achieve performance. Very often the organizational mix of identity, values, and beliefs (the fuel) doesn't align with the aspirations of employees (combustion) and makes hard work of tasks (the engine splutters) which results in poor performance (refer to figure 6.1).

There are many types of power produced by organizational cultures, and most of these emerge from one of three basic cultural orientations.

■ The authoritarian culture – *coercive power*

This is a traditional command and control culture that produces a coercive power. It identifies with hard, bottom line, results and stringent cost controls. It is a rule-maker. Its values are about position and status, who you are and what you have rather than what you can do, protocol, procedures, bureacracy, and legitimacy. Its beliefs about people tend to align behind McGregor's theory[1] – that people need to be controlled otherwise they will get away with as much as pos-

[1] Douglas McGregor, *The human side of enterprise*, McGraw-Hill, 1960.

sible. Coercive power is produced by a management of mistrust, formality, authority and with respect for higher status regardless of contribution.

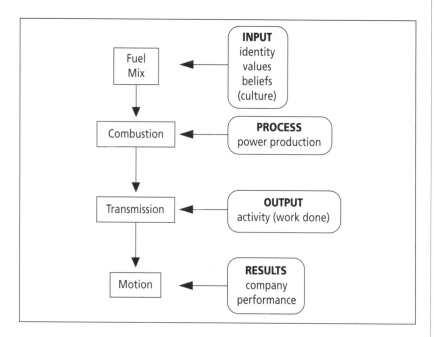

■ FIGURE 6.1
Power production

■ The technical culture – *expert power*

This culture is wrapped up in itself. It identifies with knowledge, skill, expertise and ingenuity. It is a technocrat and a judge. This culture values precision, facts, accuracy, competence, and judgment. Its beliefs about people are based on intelligence, knowledge and ingenuity. Expert power is produced by an intelligent, knowledgeable, expert management.

■ The learning culture – *generative power*

This is the culture of empowerment. It identifies with improvement, quality, change, fun, ingenuity, variety, and the future. It is a nurturer, enabler and a vehicle for achievement. When people leave it is often because they have been developed to a level at which they can only progress further in other environments. Partings are mutually agreeable and celebrated by both manager and employee.

The learning culture values individual contributions rather than position or status and it is achievement oriented. It believes that future success is dependent upon the creative contribution of its people. It produces generative power – a power that it is able to continue generating itself without regular management intervention. Its generative power is produced by a nurturing, supporting and challenging management.

Culture	Identity	Values	Beliefs	Power
Authoritarian	Rule maker Controller	Position Status Protocol Procedures Legitimacy	People need to be kept under control	Coercive
Technical	Technocrat Judge	Precision Facts Accuracy Competence Judgment	Expertise is the most important measure of people	Expert
Learning	Nurturer Achiever Enabler	Contribution Achievement Development	Future success is dependent upon the creativity of people, so empower them to make necessary changes	Generative

You will find that in reality few organizations fit exactly into one of these three cultures, but that they may have a mix of all three with one being the most predominant. For the remainder of this chapter I will focus on the learning culture, and the dynamics that produce generative power.

Conditions for producing generative power

There are some fundamental conditions that are typical of learning cultures and empowered organizations. These conditions form the system within which people can be nurtured and developed. It is also a system that has as few boundaries and constraints as possible to allow for the maximum amount of flexibility and change. Also, by virtue of empowering people, you are removing controlling influences, and this is probably one of the biggest hurdles a manager must overcome. A fundamental prerequisite for empowerment is the letting go of control mechanisms.

In my management workshops I refer to the continuum between control and empowerment. To demonstrate the importance of this I invite students to participate in a trust fall. This involves a blindfolded volunteer falling off a table backwards into the arms of colleagues who are standing at the ready. To fall confidently without bending the knees or back requires giving up control of the situation and putting your trust in your colleagues.

Trust develops as control is handed over. Many managers are afraid of the consequences of handing over control. It's not losing control, more trusting it to others who are likely to interpret the meaning of control in their own way.

A fundamental prerequisite for empowerment is the letting go of control mechanisms.

Trust develops as control is handed over.

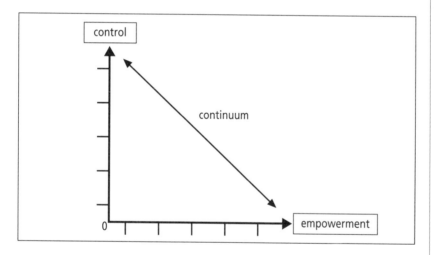

■ FIGURE 6.2
The control-empowerment continuum

Letting go of control then is the first step to trusting people, and trust is the main building block of empowerment. I like to think of it as a wheel where trust is the axle around which all the other conditions of empowerment spin. Figure 6.3 shows this as the wheel of empowerment with one condition attached to each spoke of the wheel.

The wheel is used to explain the relationship between the conditions. They are not hierarchical, pyramidal, or step relationships. Like the spokes of a wheel, each condition provides the strength to support the others – they are interdependent relationships. If you take one away, the wheel will weaken and eventually collapse. The

Trust is the main building block of empowerment.

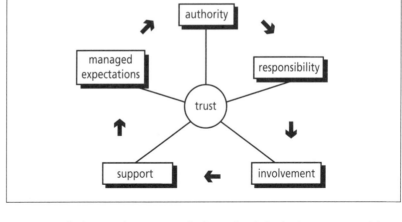

**Power is no
use without the
authority to
use it.**

position of the spokes around the wheel isn't important either. Without the spokes, the axle is an item without purpose.

There are five spokes to the wheel. Power is no use without the authority to use it. Clear guidance on the limits to authority must be given with a bias towards sufficient authority to reduce the span of control to a minimum (this will depend upon size of responsibility). In most cases this will be influenced by the decisions that need to be taken on a frequent enough basis to maintain levels of customer satisfaction.

Responsibility should also be clearly defined, specifically areas of shared responsibility. Intelligent decisions that stem from increased levels of authority and responsibility will depend upon knowledge of the business, and the best way to expand this is through involvement in the business – exposing people to new business areas and increasing their knowledge. People will want to feel supported when they are making decisions, taking risks and generally sticking their neck out.

The final spoke completes the wheel – managing people's expectations. People don't change their behavior just because you want them to. They need both intrinsic and extrinsic rewards. Whatever expectations you set, they must be manageable. This covers both expectations you have of your team (outcomes), and what they expect to get in return for investing their energy. Over-promising and under-delivering in both these areas is fatal.

Two important first lessons about empowerment

■ Lesson number one – *the easy solution*

A few years ago it was possible to occupy your working week attending short conferences on the theme of empowerment. Just about every management consultancy firm was hosting one. Managers would be attracted by the buzz words and go along for a dose of "what to do," only to find on their return to the workplace that just telling people they were being empowered to take important decisions wasn't working. Of course it wasn't – what you had to do was go back and pay the management consultants to do it for you. They knew *how* to do it. Lesson number one is people do not become empowered overnight, or by being told they are now empowered.

People do not become empowered overnight, or by being told they are now empowered.

■ Lesson number two – *my people don't want to be empowered*

I can guarantee that either at the end of my leadership workshops, or at a follow-up and integration day, at least one person will ask *"what do you do about people who don't want to be empowered?"* Well, you can't win them all, can you? For some people the penny never seems to drop about how language gives clues to our behavior. The words . . . *don't want to be empowered* . . . imply that someone has explicitly *offered* empowerment which of course isn't going to work. You do not *issue* power as the government does with the police force, rather you provide the right fuel mix (conditions) for power to be generated. There is a massive difference between the two.

Lesson number two is as follows: Make sure that your own thinking around the dynamics of empowerment is correct. Align your own levels of learning to create the conditions of empowerment and monitor feedback from your language (particularly your internal dialog). Empowerment is not something you issue or something you do to others. It is a generative condition in response to a newly formed set of values and beliefs.

Align your own levels of learning to create the conditions of empowerment.

Groups in organizations form common values and beliefs in response to the way they are treated.

NLP

A person's behavior in a situation is the best choice available to them.

NLP

Have respect for other people's maps of the world.

A question of respect

Everyone has their own set of values and beliefs which are held very close to them. Groups in organizations form common values and beliefs in response to the way they are treated. Organizations, or parts of an organization that have yet to become learning cultures and produce generative power, will have a set of values and beliefs that they have formed in response to how they have been treated in the past. If the culture had been mainly authoritarian, they may still put a value on doing as little as possible and keeping their head down below the parapet. They may believe that they have few prospects because no-one would recognize their efforts of achievement anyway. If someone did notice them it usually meant bad news about something trivial like procedures or working practices.

Values and beliefs like this become set after a while. They help to create identities of disconnectedness with the organization. When you turn up for work you become a ducker and diver. Working within a culture like this for two or three years is long enough to generate some very unproductive behaviors that are not likely to change overnight. A person's behavior in a situation is the best choice available to them. People learn the best ways of surviving in situations, and as a change agent, this is something you must learn to respect. Have respect for other people's maps of the world and you will begin to understand why they are as they are.

There is no right or wrong in human behavioral terms, only *what is*. In chapter 2 the NLP communication model explained how people's maps of the world influence their behavior, and so if you want someone to change their behavior you must offer them choices of different maps, and allow them to make their own decision to change.

■ WIIFM – *or what's in it for me?*

David McClelland, the Harvard psychologist, says that there are three requirements to change. A person has to:

- want to change;
- be allowed to change;
- know how to change.

For a person to want to change, to generate the motivation to change, there must be some reward. Intrinsic rewards of self-esteem and personal development may not be perceived as rewards if they are operating out of a world map that was designed to deal with an authoritarian culture. It may be futile to offer people a better future if their attitudes to the organization are based on a moving away from metaprogram and avoidance strategies. And how about the second requirement? If you do all the right things, will the rest of the organization still allow people to do things differently? Or will structure, bureacracy and protocol get in the way of change? I will leave the third requirement until later in this chapter where I will turn to the skills of the leader as an enabler and an agent of change. I will deal with the problem of motivation first, because if you can get to the point where people are self-motivated, and you are creating the conditions of empowerment, you are well on the way to producing generative power. Getting to this point however, takes time, patience and understanding – you need to pace identity, values and beliefs before you can begin to lead.

You need to pace identity, values and beliefs before you can begin to lead.

Pacing and leading

If you want to take people to a new place you first have to meet them where they are and respect their reasons for being there. Pacing in the business sense means being like them behaviorally in as many ways as you can without taking on the limitations that may exist for them.

For example, let's take a worst case scenario. You have taken over management of a production facility employing 250 people, 14 of whom are managers and supervisors. There is a history of poor management practice resulting in a value system of mistrust in management, dislike of trendy new "fads" such as re-engineering, which they have experienced, and a "9 to 5" mentality. The only reason for coming to work is to meet friends and earn money.

For most people this is accomplished with as little effort as possible. So, from this view you can extract that for the majority of workers, *work **means** friends and money*. This meaning is significant as you will discover in a moment after you have paced them. You will want to meet and talk with as many of them as possible – let's say you are walking around the facility and stop to talk to one of the operatives. You say to him:

> "Hi Bill. How's the new assembly run doing, is it behaving itself today?" Bill replies "it's OK. I still haven't had any joy with the requisition for the new grunging unit though – still, I should know by now not to expect too much from this outfit. They're not really interested in investment for production facilities, the bosses are too busy on foreign trips finding out the latest in Japanese working methods. They'll have us doing morning exercises next."

Now you have two options here, you can either disagree with Bill and argue with him about how things are going to change now that you are around, or you can pace his experience and get him interested in you.

> "Well Bill, I worked for one outfit that tried all the Japanese working methods (using Bill's words), and you are dead right about one thing. Sometimes bosses spend so much time looking outside the company (agreeing with Bill) that they miss what's really important inside (Implying Bill's work is important). Let me chase that requisition for you; when exactly did you post it?"

This is pacing. It is also rapport building, which I shall cover in great detail in chapter 7. By pacing people's experience you are unconsciously saying to them, "I am like you, I understand you, I have empathy with your situation, you can trust me, I have no tricks up my sleeve, you are important and your views are valid."

In a scenario like this one you will have a great deal of pacing to do whenever you make the opportunities to communicate with the 250, paying particular attention to the words you use with the management team. They may have a different set of values than the operatives. As the American critic Pauline Kael once said of culture: "One of the surest signs of the Philistine is his reverence for the superior tastes of those who put him down."

It is unsafe to assume that everyone buys into the same value system. What you are doing is pacing current state, so that you can begin to lead to some other desired state. One of the ways of re-orienting people towards a desired state is with a reframe.

Reframing

Jim Froud, an artist and poet friend of mine, demonstrated the power of reframing very simply with an elderly lady who lives close by. She was complaining that her gas bill was too high when Jim interjected with an excellent reframe which changed her entire meaning around the gas bill. He said:

> "Well, it does seem high doesn't it, especially to a pensioner with no income – but did you know that the gas company have spent millions of pounds looking for gas in the North Sea, and upon finding it they pushed a pipe deep into the sea bed and brought it 800 miles into your house, then fixed a tap onto the end – all for free? And you can choose to use it as much as you need to. In fact, you could reduce your gas bill by eating more raw fruit and vegetables and end up being healthier, couldn't you?"

What a powerful reframe!

This is what you need to do with the 250 production operatives. Work to them *means* meeting friends and earning money. I'm not suggesting that you can reframe this meaning in one sentence, as Jim did with the old lady, it takes time and patience where you have group value systems framing the meaning. But over time you will want to reframe this meaning of work to a more desired meaning – one that is more in tune with a learning culture.

A more useful and enjoyable meaning of work might be – work *means* friends, *money* and *enjoyment, learning, development, challenge, achievement.* People will make their own meaning, and so don't expect everyone to form the same meaning you have in your mind. Your job is to offer people another choice of thinking about work which requires more resourceful states of being that will begin to produce generative decision making power. And your job is no longer a decision maker or problem solver, but enabler and coach.

The empowering leader

Staying with my example of the 250 production operatives, we can begin to define in more detail the new role of the manager, or the empowering leader. Before going any further however, it is important to recognize the power of beliefs.

In chapter 1 I said that beliefs are the glue that hold values together. The change process is going to start with melting this glue, and once this process begins you will be surprised at how quickly people respond thereafter. Do you remember, in chapter 1, the psychiatric patient who believed he was a corpse? Beliefs are like self-fulfilling prophecies. You may have heard of the Pygmalion effect from Greek mythology. Pygmalion fell in love with Galatea, the beautiful statue he was carving. Aphrodite, goddess of love, took pity on him and rewarded his devotion by bringing her to life. Whatever you believe, it is true for you.

This has two important implications. First, that people will be hanging on to their existing belief systems which they have been reinforcing with their perceptual filters, and second, you will have your belief systems around these people. If you believe in them they will respond. If you do all the things you are supposed to do, but inside you are telling yourself they will not change, you are incongruent and your inner belief system will determine the outcome of your efforts – as a self-fulfilling prophecy. So, how do you enable and coach people?

■ The leader as teacher

I want you to cast aside any associations you may have of teaching that relate to chalk and talk methods, and instead take on a new meaning of teacher. These 250 operatives need to know how to change, and you are the change agent. Once they have begun to change their beliefs and take on new values, they will need the capability to change their behavior and activate the different responsibilities and authority you want them to manage. How you interact with people as their teacher will determine your level of success.

When you think of yourself as a teacher, think of drawing out knowledge rather than putting it in. When people arrive at their own conclusions and decisions they are much more committed to seeing them through than anything you can prescribe for them. Coaching is the method used to "draw out," and it does this by reflection. Before I explain coaching, in your global role as teacher, there are three main areas of focus:

How you interact with people as their teacher will determine your level of success.

1 Identifying opportunities to coach

These can come at any time. When you have established a "new culture" you may wish to introduce formal coaching sessions. However, coaching is best done as the work opportunities present themselves. Take every advantage of a coaching opportunity – if you pass up one golden opportunity, make sure your reason for doing so is fully justified. How will you spot coaching opportunities? Any time where any of the following conditions prevail:

- An employee asks you how to do something
- An employee asks you to do something
- An employee asks for your advice
- An employee says "I can't"
- You are asked for an opinion or decision
- You notice someone doing a task in an ineffective or inefficient way
- You want to broaden someone's thinking around a task
- You are participating with employees on a team task.

2 Agreeing outcomes with people

Make a habit of using well formed outcomes rather than objectives. After a while people will begin to use these as a natural process to consider consequences. I am often asked, in my role as developer, if there is a course for people to teach them about consequences. Not considering the consequences of decisions is a common cause of many problems in business. I can recall teaching outcomes to one group on a quality improvement program, and three months later heard that one student was running his life by well formed outcomes! Can you believe it? Once you believe in something you will make it work.

3 Matching individuals to tasks

Take notice of people's metaprograms and match jobs that they will get something out of. Don't put a small chunker in charge of policy making, or an options person on a task requiring lots of repetition. Business is rife with people matched with the wrong jobs, and the worrying thing is that, in many large organizations, this gets overlooked and people get trained to do jobs which they don't enjoy. If you get the right match you will then be able to stretch people by providing challenges for them.

■ The leader as coaching enabler

Coaching and enabling go inextricably together. If you are doing one, you need to be doing the other. Your outcome is to enable people to achieve more for themselves and for the organization. And you will want to achieve this by drawing out rather than putting in. There are two basic modes to effective business coaching – questioning and suggesting.

Questioning

Always find out what the employee's outcome is. This seems like common sense, and you are right, but it is possible to spend time coaching someone to achieve an outcome that has not been thoroughly thought through. Check this out first if you're not absolutely sure about it (you might want to remind yourself of the well formed conditions for outcomes by referring back to chapter 3). Having satisfied yourself that outcomes are well formed you can begin the questioning process.

I will not attempt to provide you with all the questions you will need for all possible coaching situations as this could fill an entire book in itself, but we can go back to our production operatives and imagine that we have identified a coaching opportunity with one of the line managers (Mary) who has come to you with a problem. Note that my outcome is formed around Mary's development as a manager, not around Mary's outcomes for achieving her targets. I want to develop Mary's capability to make decisions for herself rather than solve this one decision for her. So the sensory based evidence criteria for my outcome is that when I ask Mary what problems she has been having, she will tell me about specific problems, and how she has overcome them without the help of management.

Mary: *"I'm going to fall short of the target this week because I can't get the new grunger commissioned in time for tomorrow's re-tooling."*

Manager: *"Hmm. I wonder, what is your target for the week?"*

Mary: *"Two hundred units."*

Manager: *"And what do you have to make to achieve that?"*

Mary: *"Another 50 units."*

Manager: *"What have you tried so far?"*

Mary: *"I've tried telling the plant engineers of the urgency to have the new machine commissioned, but they won't listen. I can't think of what else to do. The other grungers are running to capacity."*

Manager: *"Why won't the plant engineers listen?"*

Mary: *"They're only interested in full shift work, and this job only gives them half a shift. They won't earn their full allowance on it."*

Manager: *"Well, this is worth thinking about for a while. Mary, can you imagine what would have to happen for you to meet your targets this week?"*

Mary: *"Hmmm. I've thought of everything else. The only way we're going to do it is if we get that new grunger commissioned, but I can't see the plant engineers coming over for a half shift."*

Manager: *"What can you see them coming over for?"*

> Mary: *"Well, I know it will hit our budget, but if I put in a request for maintenance on the widget sorter at the same time, I could make up a complete shift for them. The work will need to be done some time."*
>
> Manager: *"That seems like a great idea to me. Let me know how it goes."*

In all these questions the manager has not given Mary a solution. Mary came up with her own solution, which may not have been the best one, but it has succeeded in getting Mary to begin making decisions of this type on her own. Success can only be truly determined when the manager gets feedback to match sensory-based evidence criteria.

Suggesting

This should be used only where the employee is not able to form his own solution. If you have asked all the probing questions and still there is no glimmer of an idea, then offer your suggestions, but in a way that the employee almost thinks it is her solution. Here's an example using Tom from the production facility.

> Tom: *"The scrap rate is going up because we are getting contaminated raw materials."*
>
> Manager: *"That's a serious problem. What have you done about it?"*
>
> Tom: *"I can't see what I can do about it. Raw materials aren't my responsibility."*
>
> Manager: *"Well, this happened to me when I worked for ABCo, and I wasn't pleased about the way other people's quality problems were affecting my work."*
>
> Tom: *"That's how I feel, but nobody cares."*
>
> Manager: *"I wonder what would happen if someone were to write to the supplier in question, and also copy our purchasing people with the letter?"*

> Tom: *"That's not a bad idea. I would really let them know the extent of the problems we are having to deal with because of it."*
>
> Manager: *"Well, it seems like the best option open to you since no-one else seems to be looking at this serious problem."*
>
> Tom: *"Hmmm. You're right. Maybe I'll do that right now."*
>
> Manager: *"Copy me on the letter please Tom."*

These are just a couple of examples of how a coaching session might go. If you have never coached before it is well worth investing time from your portfolio into a training course. The best gift you can give your people is the gift of personal development. Modern organizations are alive with personal development opportunities – all that some people need is a good coach to get them off the starting blocks.

They say power corrupts and perhaps it does. What I know, in myself, is quite a different thing. That power corrupts the people it is exercised over.

RAYMOND WILLIAMS,
British academic

COMMUNICATION

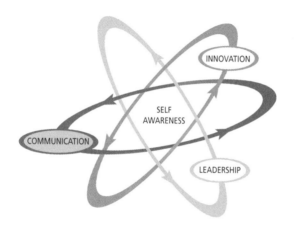

INNOVATION

SELF
AWARENESS

COMMUNICATION

LEADERSHIP

NEUROLOGICAL CHANNELS

■ **Insights to the way people think**

■ **A three part communication signal**

■ **Representation systems**

■ **The visual system**

■ **The auditory system**

■ **The kinesthetic system**

■ **Internal dialogue**

■ **Submodalities**

Preferred representation system / Lead representation system / Visual language / Visual eye movements / Visual breathing, gestures, and vocal qualities / Auditory language / Auditory eye movements / Auditory breathing, gestures, and vocal qualities / Kinesthetic language / Kinesthetic eye movements / Kinesthetic breathing, gestures, and vocal qualities

Insights to the way people think

In chapter 1, if you recall, I said that ultimate flexibility will be realized when you begin to respond to behavioral patterns and processes rather than to the content of a situation, and I referred to a range of different meetings where communication skills would be needed. This chapter will take you further down that route by showing you ways in which you can respond to someone's process, or pattern of thinking, rather than to the content of what they are saying. That is not to say that content is irrelevant, but that it is more useful to respond to the process than it is to the content. If you know the process of a communication, you are better able to respond in an appropriate style to achieve an agreeable outcome.

At a macro level, a colleague at a meeting might say: "I have noticed that sales of blue widgets have taken a dive again." In this example, if you were responsible for blue widgets you might respond in a number of ways to this comment. You might be defensive and say "this was anticipated with the current market trends" in which case you have merely reacted to the content with the sole intention of defending yourself. You might be more detailed with your answer and say "yes, we're down exactly three percent from the budgeted sales figure which is a six percent year to date adverse variance" in which case you are still reacting to the content of the discussion.

If you know the process of a communication, you are better able to respond in an appropriate style to achieve an agreeable outcome.

A better response would be to identify the process before providing information, for example: "perhaps, but I would be interested to know how relevant this is to the matter in hand, and whether at this stage, it helps to flush out the issues we are all here to resolve." This reply invites the questioner to assess their own thought process and justify the relevance of the statement. This is just one example to demonstrate the difference between content and process at the macro level. Politicians are experts in working with the process of a discussion regardless of content.

Politicians are experts in working with the process of a discussion regardless of content.

In chapter 8 you will be introduced to the linguistic techniques which the best politicians use when they are working with the process. This chapter will continue to explore the processes at the micro level of human communication to build even more flexibility into your thinking and behavior.

If communication in organizations is to become more productive, it must start at the level of trust and understanding. Trust is a fundamental prerequisite for creating a culture of empowerment, and people will reciprocate trust only when they believe managers understand them and their problems. Without understanding and trust, people are very sceptical and suspicious of change. By understanding how people communicate at the micro level, we are able to match our own patterns of communication more closely to the patterns of others and so develop deep rapport, understanding, and trust.

Rapport is one of the fundamental requirements for productive communication which is based on the principle well known to all successful sales people – *people like people who are like them.* It is very rare that a person will buy either a product, idea or suggestion from someone they even slightly dislike. This chapter provides much of the micro-level communication patterns you will need to develop deep rapport with anyone.

People will reciprocate trust only when they believe managers understand them and their problems.

A three part communication signal

As a communicator, having an insight to the way people think gives you some distinct advantages. Recognizing patterns of thought can help you to develop deep levels of rapport, understanding, trust and friendship while also exerting influence over the way your ideas and proposals are received. From the micro patterns you can access much more of a person's total message than from the words alone.

Research has shown that whenever we communicate, only 7 percent of our message is contained in the words. Thirty-eight percent is contained in the tone of voice, and 55 percent is contained in body language, or the neurological channel. Human communication is interpreted through this three part signal, and it is the unconscious mind that will pick up the non-verbal part of a message even if your conscious mind misses it. If you were to say to one of your employees "I'm comfortable with you taking three months to complete this project," but you know there is pressure on you to complete it earlier, your body and tone of voice will supply the majority of the

**Words = 7%
Tone of voice = 38%
Physiology = 55%**

message. In this case it will be incongruent to the words you are saying and the employee will unconsciously pick up this 93 percent of your message which is saying "I am not *really* comfortable with this."

The employee could be left confused because of your incongruence. Being able to notice the non-verbal elements of someone's communication is the first step to understanding their thinking process. Responding to it in a flexible way is the second step. Here you will learn about the neurological channels of communication before proceeding to the linguistic channels in chapter 8.

Representation systems

We represent information internally by way of pictures, sounds, feelings, smells and tastes. Think of it as representing inside our minds that which we take in through our five senses from the external territory (refer to figure 2.2, chapter 2). Our senses are our information input channels. As I look out of my window I notice the leaves falling from the trees, and I can hear a dog barking in the distance. As my thoughts turn to the feeling of hunger in my stomach from the smell of dinner roasting in the oven, the taste of parsnips in my mouth completes the feeling that fall has arrived, and I tell myself that summer is over for another year.

Did you follow the route of my sensory experience? Did you see leaves falling from the trees? Could you taste the parsnips? Whatever we take in from the external territory we represent internally by a mix of all our senses. This multi-sensory input influences our thought processing. Have you ever woken up in the morning after having a vivid dream that seemed real? Many people experience dreams that are so vivid they have difficulty knowing what was real and what was part of a dream. This is because the brain constructs real and imagined experiences in the same way, with the same chemical reactions. Our reality is what we represent in our mind from the external world around us.

Our representational systems influence our thinking, and over time we develop preferences in the way we use them. In the western world the primary representation systems are visual, auditory and kinesthetic. The olfactory (smell) and gustatory (taste) systems are more often used as triggers to the other systems. The smell of dinner roasting triggers a feeling of hunger. In the eastern world you will find that smell and taste are more commonly used as primary systems than in the west, although many westerners may find this a difficult concept to understand.

■ Preferred representation system

People think in all three primary representation systems and most people have a preference for one over the other two. The preferred system will be the one that is the most developed and the one with which fine distinctions can be made.

You will find that experts who demonstrate their skill with ease and excellence are able to make many fine distinctions in the relevant representation systems. Dancers, for example, will have a well developed sense of feeling to help guide their movement. Artists will have a well developed visual system, and musicians a strong auditory system.

You will also find people in all kinds of disciplines with differing mixes of strengths in each system. Auditory people "like the sound" of an idea while a visual person would "see the potential" and a kinesthetic might "have a warm feeling" about it. The systems that are not used as often as the preferred system often explain why a person experiences difficulty in acquiring certain skills. Someone with an underdeveloped auditory facility will not find learning the piano as easy a task as would a person with a preference for the auditory system.

■ Lead representation system

Many people have what is called a lead system, which is the system used to access past experiences from memory. Once a memory has been brought into conscious thought by the lead system, the preferred system takes over to recall the finer distinctions from the experience. For example, if I were to ask you how your most recent meeting went you might first access a picture you have stored of the people at the meeting, then you might *tune in* to the discussion. In this example, the visual system was the lead to the preferred auditory system.

Once a memory has been brought into conscious thought by the lead system, the preferred system takes over to recall the finer distinctions from the experience.

Some people have a kinesthetic lead system which accesses stored feelings from memory in order to recreate either visual images or sounds from an experience. Other people lead with the visual system and hand over to kinesthetic for the finer distinctions of how they felt about an experience. A master chef will have a well developed sense of smell and taste with which to make fine distinctions about the meals he prepares.

It is useful to recognize the differences and be able to identify, from certain behavioral cues, how a person is thinking. The aim is not to stereotype people as auditories, visuals or kinesthetics; that isn't so useful – it's about noticing how someone is thinking at any moment in time, and there are more than enough cues to help us do this from sensory-based language, eye movements, breathing patterns, gestures, and voice qualities.

The visual system

People with a well developed visual system think in pictures. Their memories will contain more visual detail than feelings or sounds, and they will more readily describe how people or things looked than what was said or how they were feeling at the time. Their visual distinctions will be richer and more detailed than those of an auditory or kinesthetic person. Generalizing experience from the NLP training community reveals that about 35 percent of the population have a preference for the visual representation system.

■ Visual language

The words people use give strong clues to their preferred system of representation. For example, a person with a well developed visual system might say: "I would like a *clearer view* of this project. The *picture* I have is much too *hazy* for me to make a decision." The term for these sensory-based words is "predicates." In the every-day jargon of management there are certain sensory-based words, or predicates that are give-aways to a person's preferred system, such as "get a *perspective* on the problem" or "*see* the project through." Here are some more examples of visual predicates that a visually oriented person might often use:

Thirty-five per cent of the population have a preference for the visual representation system.

"The future's sketchy."	"That's one way of looking at it."
"Let me picture this."	"That's a bright idea."
"I've seen one aspect of this."	"It's not at all clear."
"We can see eye to eye."	"Let's focus on the issues."
"That's a dim view to take."	"It's a sight for sore eyes."
"I see what you mean."	"Let me reveal the plan."
"It shows promise."	"Let me shed some light on this."
"Beyond a shadow of a doubt."	"It's been well scoped out."

■ Visual eye movements

If you watch people's eyes as they are talking you will notice many movements – up, down, laterally, fixed frontal gazes and many other combinations. Research has shown that these eye movements correspond to how we are accessing or processing information. There is a direct neurological link between the eye movements and the different parts of the brain that are used for different types of thinking. When people are thinking visually their eyes will be either upward or focussed on some point in space straight ahead. Right-handed people look up – to the left when they are recalling past experiences, and up – to the right when they are constructing an image for the first time.

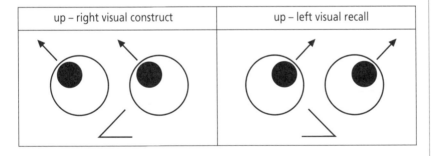

up – right visual construct	up – left visual recall

■ FIGURE 7.1
Eye accessing cues – visual representation system

Most left-handed people have a reversed left/right configuration. Once an image has been constructed or recalled, it is sometimes placed more centrally for further processing. This is the forward gaze. Try this out for yourself – pose to someone the following questions and requests while you watch their eye movements. Watch closely as the movements are often very quick and darting.

1 I want you to imagine what a green monkey would look like riding on the back of a blue elephant dressed in a pink ballet costume.

What you might expect to see is a move up – left to get the pictures of the real animals, then a move up – right to construct the peculiar image of them all together.

2 What was the design of your bedroom wallpaper you had as a child?

This should get you a move up – left.

3 What were you doing at this time of day, five days ago?

You should get another up – left movement.

What did you find? Don't worry if you got lots of lateral and downward movements as well, these relate to other modes of thought which I will cover shortly. When you know what all the eye movements mean you will be able to practice reading them. If you want to develop your visual system use these eye movements to assist your thinking.

■ Visual breathing, gestures, and vocal qualities

Visually oriented people tend to centre their breathing high in the chest area, and it is more shallow and at a faster rate than the breathing of auditories and kinesthetics. Many NLP techniques are based on the visual system because, for the majority of people, it is the most effective system to work with for creating personal change. Some people may experience difficulty making pictures in their mind. If you should happen to be among this category with an under developed visual system, you will find that matching the attributes that are associated with visual thinking will assist you to construct richer visual images.

When people are thinking visually they gesture upwards with their head, arms and hands. Look at the photographs and paintings of any well known visionary and you will find that in the majority of pictures they are gesturing upward in some way. When I recall pictures of Martin Luther King for example, it is with his arms raised upward as if helping to recreate his "dream."

Visual gestures may be exaggerated arm, head, and body movements or they may be more discreet than that – fingers pointing upward is one example. Visual thinking also has some distinct vocal characteristics. When a person is thinking in the visual mode they tend to speak quickly to keep up with all the pictures their mind is creating, and their voice pitch is high in relation to that of auditory and kinesthetic modes of thinking.

The auditory system

People who have a preference for the auditory system are able to make finer distinctions in sound than in pictures or feelings. They will often recall the precise words people used in meetings or presentations, but they may not recall so easily the color of the room, the clothes worn by the presenter, or how they felt at the time. They are also more likely to remember vocal characteristics and any background noise. Auditory people are often easily distracted by sounds around them since their perceptual filters are tuned in to listen in preference to seeing and feeling. Generalizing experience from the NLP training community reveals that around 20 percent of the population prefer the auditory system.

Experience from the NLP training community reveals that around 20 percent of the population prefer the auditory

■ Auditory language

Some examples of auditory predicates in commonly used phrases are:

"I hear you."   "Could you amplify that statement?"
"Let me tune in to this."   "Music to my ears."
"Sounds like a great idea." "He's playing the wrong tune."
"Describe it to me."   "I would like to comment."
"That rings a bell."   "I'll echo that."
"I'm all ears."   "That's a loud statement."
"It's hush hush."   "We're in harmony over this."
"We're on the same   "It's loud and clear."
   wavelength."   "Say it word for word."
"In a manner of speaking."

■ Auditory eye movements

When people think in sounds their eyes move laterally left or right. A lateral left move indicates remembered sounds and lateral right constructed sounds.

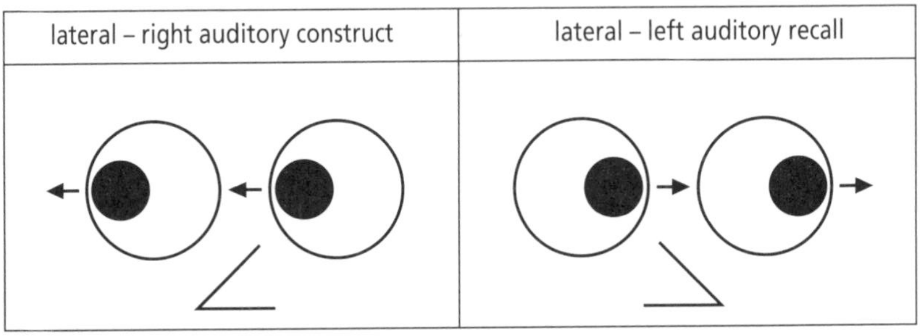

lateral – right auditory construct	lateral – left auditory recall

■ FIGURE 7.2
Eye accessing cues – auditory representation system

Try the following requests out on people you know:

1 I want you to recite the Lord's Prayer.
  This should bring about a move laterally to the left.

2 I want you to make up a short, instrumental, tune.
  This should cause a move laterally to the right.

If you stimulated other movements either in addition to, or instead of, the lateral moves, it could mean that your subject used a kinesthetic or visual lead system, or was extremely weak in the auditory system. For example, a strong visual person might have seen themselves reading the Lord's Prayer at some specific time in their past. When you practice with other people be sure to give requests rather than ask questions. Invariably if you ask someone "can you recite the Lord's Prayer?" they will answer "yes" without checking if they really can remember it the whole way through. By giving requests, or commands, your subject is more inclined to search for the information and you will notice the eye movements.

■ Auditory breathing, gestures, and vocal qualities

Auditory breathing expands the whole chest area. The head is usually in a well balanced position, or sometimes leaning to one side as if listening to something. Gestures may consist of touching the ears, or more generally, making rhythmic movements with whole or parts of the body. Swaying rhythmically on the feet is characteristic of auditory thinking. The voice is usually quite rich with a good tonal range and plenty of resonance.

The kinesthetic system

When people are thinking kinesthetically they are accessing feelings. They prefer to "get a feel" for something rather than hear about it or look at a picture. When assessing project timescales they are more inclined to go with a "feeling" about the amount of time allocated than make a decision based upon what they read from a project plan. About 45 percent of the population use the kinesthetic system as their primary system.

■ Kinesthetic language

The following are examples of kinesthetic predicates in commonly used phrases :

"I like the feel of that."
"Start again from scratch."
"Bite the bullet."
"Smooth out the problems."
"I'll get in touch with you."
"I get your drift."
"Get a handle on this."
"Let's firm up on this."
"Can you grasp this idea."
"Dig deep and you'll find it."
"We need to move on this one."
"Keep your shirt on."
"Touch base with me."

"Whip up a storm."
"You can feel the pressure."
"It's based on concrete
   evidence."
"Hang in there."
"I can feel it in my bones."
"He's thick-skinned."
"We've only scratched
   the surface."
"It was a heated discussion."
"You can sense what's
   happening."

■ Kinesthetic eye movements

The eye-accessing cue of a kinesthetic thought process is down and to the right. This is where the eyes go when you want to get in touch with a feeling which could be an internal emotion, or an external tactile feeling.

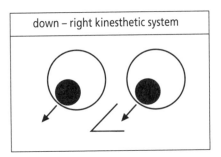

■ FIGURE 7.3
Eye accessing
cues – kinesthetic
representation
system

Try the following requests/questions out on people you know:

1 I want you to imagine what it feels like to have wet clothing next to your skin.

2 How do you feel when you are really relaxed?

You will find that most people use their kinesthetic system to check how they feel about certain things. If you found that some people looked laterally or upward, it could be that they have an under-developed kinesthetic system. Have you ever heard people complaining about their "unfeeling" partners?

■ Kinesthetic breathing, gestures, and vocal qualities

When people are thinking kinesthetically they breathe deeper and much lower in the abdomen compared to visual and auditory breathing. Gestures are often inextricably linked with speech although mainly limited to the lower part of the body area. The head is often angled down, and the voice tone is deeper. Speech is slower than with auditory and visual thinking, with frequent pauses to check how they are feeling about what they are saying and what they want to say.

Internal dialog

Talking with oneself is another way of thinking. People who have developed a preference for this type of thinking often seem distant from a conversation for long periods because they need to have internal conversations with themselves to make decisions. This is a very time-consuming decision making process compared to the visual system where decisions can be made as fast as you are able to flash comparative visuals through your mind's eye. The eye position that gives the cue for internal dialog is down – left.

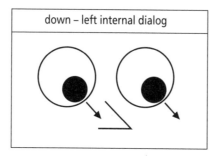

down – left internal dialog

■ FIGURE 7.4
Eye accessing cues –
Internal dialog.

The gesture that is normally associated with internal dialog is known as the "telephone position" with one hand on the side of the face, the index finger pointing towards the ear, middle finger under the nose, and thumb under the chin. People who do most of their thinking by internal dialog usually read by repeating the written word in their own dialog. This is a very slow and ineffective way of reading compared with a visual strategy which translates the words into pictures at a much faster pace than dialog can ever hope to achieve. You can, however, add an extra dimension to novels by using different internal voices for the characters.

When you begin to notice how people are thinking, remember – there is no right or wrong way to think. If someone doesn't seem able to think visually, that is how they have learned to operate in the world. It is by interpreting the cues for how people are thinking, that we are able to significantly improve the productivity of communication.

Try this exercise to ascertain your preferred representation system:

Remember – there
is no right or
wrong way to
think.

Representation system questionnaire

 EXERCISE 7

For each of the following questions there are three answers. Choose the one answer that seems most natural to you. Do this quickly spending no more than a few seconds on each question.

1 When you first learn of a new project do you prefer to initially . . .
   (a) See the big picture?

(b) Talk it over with yourself or others?

(c) Get a feel for how it might unfold?

2 When you come up against problems do you prefer to . . .

    (a) Bounce ideas around?

    (b) Imagine different perspectives?

    (c) Talk through the options?

3 When you celebrate successes do you prefer to . . .

    (a) Broadcast the news?

    (b) Project a bright picture for everyone to see?

    (c) Give everyone a pat on the back?

4 When negotiating do you prefer to . . .

    (a) Debate the options?

    (b) Imagine the possibilities?

    (c) Take a flexible stance?

5 At company seminars do you prefer to . . .

    (a) Grasp the gist of the message?

    (b) Hear the message word for word?

    (c) Sketch out the meaning?

6 During meetings do you prefer to . . .

    (a) Observe the views of others?

    (b) Tune in to other people's remarks?

    (c) Feel the thrust of the arguments?

7 When brainstorming do you prefer to . . .

    (a) Take a bird's-eye view of the situation?

    (b) Thrash ideas around?

    (c) Voice suggestions?

8 When traveling to work do you prefer to . . .

    (a) Get a feel for how your day will go?

    (b) Focus on the day ahead?

    (c) Talk over your daily schedule?

9 When you need information do you prefer to . . .

    (a) Talk to an expert?

    (b) Seek a specialist's view?

    (c) Use the experience of others?

10 When being challenged do you prefer to . . .
   (a) Sound out the other person?
   (b) Get a sense of the other person's standpoint?
   (c) Illustrate the other person's point of view?

11 When you are interviewing for new staff do you prefer to . . .
   (a) Examine all aspects of their potential?
   (b) Inquire about the comment in their C.V?
   (c) Get a firm grasp of their experience?

12 When you are preparing to write a proposal do you prefer to . . .
   (a) Cut a rough draft?
   (b) Articulate the main topics?
   (c) Clarify the overall picture?

To score your answers, put a 1 in the box next to each answer you have chosen, and leave the other two answer boxes blank.

SCORE SHEET						
		Column 1		Column 2		Column 3
1	a		b		c	
2	b		c		a	
3	b		a		c	
4	b		a		c	
5	c		b		a	
6	a		b		c	
7	a		c		b	
8	b		c		a	
9	b		a		c	
10	c		a		b	
11	a		b		c	
12	c		b		a	
TOTALS						

Interpreting your score

Column 1 contains visual modality answers, Column 2 auditory and Column 3 kinesthetic. The column with the highest score is very likely to indicate your preferred representation system. This is a very quick and simple test with no real validation data. It is always better to learn from subjective experience than it is from any contrived test. It can, however, help to *focus your listening* in the right *direction* until you *get* more of a *feel* for representation system cues.

Submodalities

Imagine for a moment that you are walking barefoot along a tropical island beach. Notice the waves gently lapping around your feet, and observe the palm trees gently swaying in a warm breeze as the sound of Carribean music in the distance harmonizes with the rhythm of your pace. What kind of picture does this create in your mind as you imagine what it would be like? Do you have a color picture or is it a black and white one? Is it a moving picture? In which location in your mind's eye is it constructed? How large is it? Is it a bright picture, or a dim one? How about the contrast?

These picture qualities are submodalities of the visual representation system. You were introduced to submodalities with the Swish technique in chapter 2 where you learned that bright colorful pictures are more motivating than dull black and white ones. Now let's go back to your beach movie. Did you hear the music, and the waves, lapping around your feet? Could you feel your feet sinking into the sand?

The auditory and kinesthetic systems have submodalities also, and there is no definitive list, only what you are able to subjectively experience. I have met people who have blue feelings and others with multi-colored sounds. I'm not going to question that – it's their world inside their neurology, not mine!

Submodalities have a direct link with the intensity of our experience. One way of experimenting with your submodalities is to imagine a control panel with a sliding control knob for each analog submodality (those that can vary over a range like dark to bright), and an on/off switch for each digital submodality (those that can only be in one of two states like color to black and white). How does

Submodalities have a direct link with the intensity of our experience.

it feel to have control over your own mind at this level? Many people accept the same old movies with the same old sound tracks re-run after re-run. Your internal dialog doesn't have to take over either – you can tame that one and get rid of the old tape loops that seem to run whenever they feel like it.

The next time you become aware of internal dialog that you would rather not have, move it to another location. Turn down the volume; turn it off; or change the tone or pitch and find out what happens. A common NLP cure for insomnia due to incessant internal dialogue (this is very common amongst workaholics) is to move the voice to another location, reduce the volume, lower the tone and make it lethargic. Try this the ne x . t   t . i . . m . . e   y . . o . . . u h . . . a . . . v . . . . e   I . . . n . . . . s . . . . . o . . . . m . . . . .

Submodalities influence your state. Remember how in step three of the sixth strategy state exercise (chapter 4) I created a *visual* of looking like a professional project manager and a *feeling* of being a professional project manager? I used submodalities to build a new part for my identity that could be a successful project manager. Even with all the knowledge about how to perform a task, or a role, if the neurological state does not allow certain distinctions to be made, performance will be limited.

Submodalities influence your state.

A common example of this can be found where high-ranking office-based administrators take on a responsibility for people and attempt to communicate with them using the submodalities they have developed for managing physical resources and using the telephone. You often get unhappy people because the administrator isn't able to make the distinctions in the visual and auditory system that are needed to understand people and communicate with them in pro-ductive ways. The key to working with your own submodalities is to:

1 Find out what your own preferred and lead representation systems are.

   Listen to the predicates you use, check how you breathe and notice your voice qualities. Ask a friend to watch your eye move-ments. You could set up your own complete test with the help of a friend.

2 Be aware of your own behavior and recognize from the feedback

you get where you need to make changes.

Where would you like to have better choices and improve the results you get?

3 Notice from your own cues what representation systems you are using to produce the behavior.

Be fully aware of how your state changes as you begin to think about these situations. Which system leads you into the preferred system you use in each of these situations?

4 Use your control panel to change your submodalities, or to change representation systems completely.

Find the critical submodality and change it in some way. If you don't know the most critical one you can start by making any change. If one change doesn't work, try another, and another.

Here's a list of some of the more common submodalities in each of the three main representation systems.

Visual submodalities

Associated or dissociated
Color or black and white
Location
Size
Size of yourself (in the picture) in relation to the overall image
Framed or panoramic
Brightness
Contrast

Depth (two or three dimensional)
Transparent or opaque
Orientation (tilt, angle)
The number of different images
Moving or still
Speed of movement
Focus
Magnification of separate objects

Auditory submodalities

Volume
Location of sounds
Words or other sounds or both
Stereo or mono
Tone

Duration
Clarity
Pitch
Resonance

Kinesthetic submodalities

Pressure	Shape
Location	Texture
Weight	Temperature
Local or whole body sensation	Intensity

To complete the picture of the micro level components of communication, the next chapter will give you a feel for the linguistic channel of communication. The spoken content of our message that constitutes a mere 7 percent of our meaning can have a significant impact when delivered with congruent physiological signals.

Half our mistakes in life arise from feeling where we ought to think, and thinking where we ought to feel.

J CHURTON COLLINS
(1848–1908)
English author, critic,
scholar

THE POWER OF SPEECH

- **Intention, purpose and outcome**
- **Language as a filter on experience**
- **Chunk size**
- **Artfully vague language**
- **Information frames**
- **Reframing**
- **Metaphor**
- **Congruence**

The Metal Model / Nominalizations / Unspecified nouns / Unspecified verbs / Lost performative / Comparisons / Mind reading / Cause and effect / Complex equivalence / Presupposition / Universal quantifiers / Generalizations / Modal operator of necessity / Modal operator of possibility / Ecology frame / Outcome frame / Relevancy challenge frame / Evidence frame / As-if frame / Backtrack frame

Words are like the warhead of a nuclear missile.

All communication has a power rating.

Language is our universal system for communicating meaning, understanding and experience to each other, and although the origins of language lie further in history than can be traced, it still can be held responsible for many of the human relations problems in modern organizations.

When the subject of communication is debated in organizations it is generally with these words in mind. *What shall we tell them? Who should we tell? How should we tell them?* In the last chapter I said that the words account for only 7 percent of meaning, and yet it is with this small amount that we can pack tremendous power into our communication. Words are like the warhead of a nuclear missile which is but a small component of the offensive submarine. Although the sight of the submarine itself may pose a striking threat, it is the warhead inside the missile that does the damage.

You may have experienced, as I have, the fall of good people through the power of the tongue, whether it be directly at the tongue of an authoritarian, unfeeling despot, or more indirectly by a leader unable to represent the true thoughts of others. All communication has a power rating, and this chapter contains many ways in which you can increase the rating of your communication to ecologically accomplish your outcomes.

Language is a tool that can be used to apply leverage to situations and help you move toward your goals. It is a diagnostic tool, and it is a tool of influence and persuasion. It provides clues to the thinking patterns and processes of others, and the way you use it can either constrain or enhance your flexibility. There are people who have become experts in the art of the "sophistry response" which was introduced in chapter 1, using highly technical words to produce solutions that seem credible at first, but become the target for sabotage because of an unconsidered group value. There are others known for being more effective than this who seem to have an enlightened awareness of the power of words. These people have learned the language of the "curiosity response." You may know people in both these categories.

Intention, purpose, and outcome

Language is one of the perceptual filters that generalize, distort and delete sensory information and help to form our own unique version of reality. Language conforms to a specific structure and a set of rules which help to sequence words so that we can be understood by others, and these rules are so deeply embedded into our unconscious that thought and speech are almost synthesized into one process. I am going to introduce you to a set of rules that will guide you to a more productive use of language, and I will start with intention and purpose.

Whenever we are opening our mouths words might be coming out, and once they're out it's too late to change them – if only it were possible to backtrack and choose our words more wisely, we could significantly improve our communication skill. Words have an instant effect on the people listening. A classic example that demonstrates this point is the person who says "People who tow trailers behind their cars are a nuisance on the road," to which a listener replies "I tow a trailer," and the first speaker responds with "Well, they're not all nuisances, it's mainly the large commercial caravans that I protest about."

The initial words that were uttered would have an effect on the listener. Do you think the listener will believe the first statement or the second? Words must be chosen wisely. Communication is effective when it is designed to achieve a higher purpose than any one individual statement, and when there is also a clear intention behind the use of each word. All communication has an intention behind it, but often we find the intention may not be a useful one, or unconscious so that the speaker is unaware of it. Some people seem to talk incessantly about all kinds of things with apparently no productive intention other than to fill space with words. An engineering manager I used to know would hijack any meeting by talking almost non-stop. His continual banter was a commentary of his experiences which quickly digressed from the business in hand. There was clearly no conscious effort to produce words with higher intentions and purpose.

I can only guess that the intention of his autopilot was perhaps to convince others of the depth of his experience. If you have no conscious intention, your autopilot will decide one for you which may be incongruent with your goals.

Thought and speech are almost synthesized into one process.

All communication has an intention behind it.

If you have no conscious intention, your autopilot will decide one for you which may be incongruent with your goals.

Language as a filter on experience

If we understand where language lets us down, we will know where to begin looking to improve communication. The NLP model of communication in chapter 2 explained how language filters experience. If I were to tell you about a recent trip I made to Germany, filling in every moment of my experience – the size, shape, color of the hotel, the type of windows it had, all my conversations with waiters, the weather each day etc – you would become bored very quickly. So I select what I consider you might be interested to know and leave out the rest.

NLP

The words we use are not the event or the item they

We do this all the time, and often the words we use to create brevity actually change the meaning of our original thoughts by generalizing, deleting and distorting the original memory. Language can be thought of as the surface structure of our experience, and the thoughts that produced the language are the deeper structure. Words can never be the original experience they seek to represent – they are too far removed from it. First we have an experience which we represent with our internal representation systems, and when we want to talk to others about the experience we recall the sensory information from memory (thoughts) which produce words. The words we use are not the event or the item they represent.

Let's take a look at some ways to upgrade the power rating of our communication, and then in the next two chapters you can discover how to put the techniques to use in a range of management activities.

Chunk size

Communication takes place on different levels. See how many different levels you can detect in this conversation amongst a group of accountants.

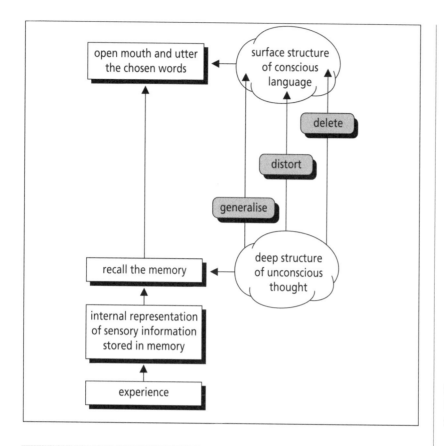

■ FIGURE 8.1
Surface and deep
structure

Jim: *"Year end results look promising."*
Ken: *"They would look even better if we could cut our sta-
         tionery costs."*
Sarah: *"Never mind stationery costs, do you know what we get
         charged for a three minute phone call?"*
Kim: *"The phone companies are making huge profits on inter-
         national business."*

Talking in large information chunks is talking more globally and
generally, while talking in small information chunks is being more
specific. If we were to talk about transport, *the transport system* is a
large chunk (global), and *the bus that takes me to work* is a small
chunk (specific). You may recall from chapter 4 a metaprogram based
on this concept.

If you were to draw a chart of the changing levels, it might look like this:

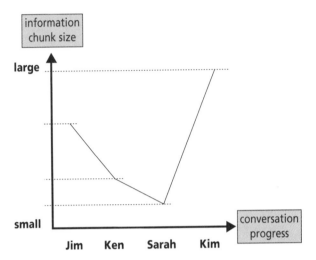

Some people prefer to speak globally, while others prefer to be specific. Flexible communication requires the ability to chunk up, down or laterally depending upon the situation. Just staying at one level is certainly inflexible. Politicians are experts at this. If you were to ask a politician a relatively small chunk question like "what are you going to do about income tax?", a common evasive response would be to chunk upward, i.e. "income tax is but one element in the inflation equation which we have always said will remain at the top of the political agenda for some years to come, and our record over the past five years clearly demonstrates that we have got it right."

This response chunked up from *income tax* to *inflation*. A lateral move remains at the same chunk size. Figure 8.2 demonstrates all three moves – up, down and lateral with the question that triggers the move in each direction.

Generally speaking you find that the more senior you are in the organization the larger the chunk size of your conversations. I have known some very senior managers who seemed to prefer communicating in small chunks. You will find that this behavior leads to an employee perception that the boss is interfering in their jobs. When you speak with managers who are more senior than you, chunk up from where you normally speak and only chunk down when they move first. When you speak to people less senior than you, chunk down slightly so they can understand you better.

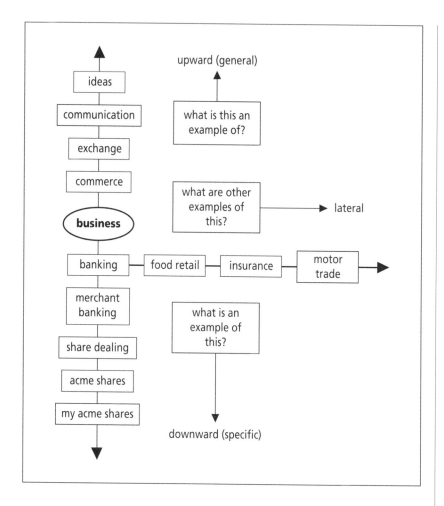

■ FIGURE 8.2
Stepping up, down
and laterally

If you are addressing a large group of people it is often best to keep your information to a large chunk size and avoid specifics. This allows people to make their own meaning of your generalizations, and you will also avoid getting tied up with specific details and technicalities. Chunking up will help you to create direction for your team by defining global objectives for the business. Once you have described these it's just a matter of chunking down until you reach the level at which your part of the organization operates.

Writing a user guide for a computer system on the other hand requires small chunk specific detail. Be aware of your own preference for chunk size, and notice the preferences of other people. Developing your ability to move up, down and across will increase the flexibility of your communication.

Artfully vague language

If you chunk up and stay there, your conversations will become "artfully vague." This is the language of presidents, politicians, professional orators, hypnotherapists and CEOs. It is the language that Hitler, Martin Luther King and Gandhi all used to achieve their very different aims. Artfully vague language is a powerful language. It is powerful because it uses words that have no specific meaning yet which anyone can believe. It makes use of gross generalizations, deletions, and distortions to remove all specific content from the message.

Company mission statements are built from artfully vague language so that they can have meaning for the whole organization. If mission statements were specific they would be so lengthy no-one would take any notice of them. Consider one of the shortest mission statements ever – "we aim to be number one." It doesn't say very much at all, but its meaning can permeate through the organization being interpreted by each person in their own way. Artfully vague language is known as the Milton Model[1] in NLP after the late Milton Erickson who was recognized around the world for his success and uniqueness as a hypnotherapist.

[1] Grinder, Bandler and DeLozier, *Patterns of the hypnotic techniques of Milton H. Erickson, MD*, Vols I and II, Meta Publications, 1975, 1976.

■ The Meta Model

The Meta Model is the antidote to artfully vague language. Clearly there will be many times where specificity is required, such as a group problem-solving session where measurement is an important criteria. The Meta Model provides the tests to recover information which has been generalized, distorted and deleted by our perceptual filters. It is known as the precision tool and is often likened to a surgeon's scalpel cutting in precisely the right place and dissecting to remove diseased tissue.

There will be times when you will want to be artfully vague, speaking at a large convention or sending a note of commendation to a company division for example. There will be other times when you will want to use the Meta Model to pin people down to specifics, such as in a problem-solving group where measurement is being defined. I will run through each of the Milton Model language patterns and give the Meta Model test with an example for each one.

■ Nominalizations

Take the word "flexibility," which is a familiar word to you by now, and ask ten people from your organization what it means to them. I guarantee you will get ten different answers (and some may well surprise you). The word "flexibility" belongs to a category of words called "nominalizations" which are process words that have been changed into nouns; i.e. to "flex" (process) and the state of "flexibility" (noun). Using words like this allows people to add their own meaning, from their own model of the world. Here's a nominalized speech . . .

"I have a great *admiration* and *respect* for the Southern team whose *delivery* of our new system has set new standards of *performance* and redefined what *success* means to our company. (The words in italics are nominalizations.)"

Now here are the Meta Model responses to this which result from changing the noun back into a process . . .

- How do you admire them?
- How do you show your respect?
- How did they deliver and to whom did they deliver?
- How exactly did they perform?
- Who or what did they succeed?

■ Unspecified nouns

This pattern deletes specific "who" and "what" information as in the following examples . . .

"They will have it ready by next Tuesday."
"The entire project was chaotic from beginning to end."
"Managers should lead from the front."
"Accountants shouldn't be trusted with these matters."

And the Meta Model responses . . .

- Who will have it ready?
- Which project? What was chaotic about it?
- Which managers? Who or what should they lead? Whose front?
- Which accountants shouldn't be trusted? What matters?

■ Unspecified verbs

This is simply a deletion of the "how" information, for example:

"We launched the product."
"The order was finally completed."
"We are doing our best."
"We are taking an aggressive approach in this marketplace."

And the Meta Model responses . . .

- How specifically did you launch the product?
- How specifically was the order completed?
- How precisely are you doing your best?
- How explicitly are you taking an aggressive approach?

■ Lost performative

These are value judgments and you can notice them in just about every sentence uttered by a politician. Examples are: "it's absolutely clear that we got this policy right;" "the future of this industry is secure;" "we have the best health system in the western world." These statements are all judgments that can have an enormous impact when used in a high level address or presentation. If you consider any dispute where the parties involved have different values, you will hear an abundance of lost performatives.

The British coal industry is a classic case, where on the one side you have miners saying "coal is still the cheapest form of fuel in the UK," and the government saying "mining is a high cost industry compared to other forms of energy production." The challenge is to ask "who says it is?" Here are some more examples . . .

"We have the best IT system on the market today."
"Our service is falling behind our competitors."
"It's obvious that what we need to do is diversify."
"She's clearly out in front of the rest."

And the Meta Model responses . . .

- According to whom?
- Who says so?

- It's obvious to whom?
- To whom is it clear she is out in front?

■ Comparisons

One of our human traits is the ability to make comparisons. We continually look around us for similarities or differences. This is a fundamental part of our brain's processing function. Yet often, in conversation, part of the information we use for comparison gets left out. Here are some examples . . .

"It's better to take this approach."
"You'll find the sales are increasing significantly."
"We're the best team for the job."
"She's an ideal candidate."

And the Meta Model responses . . .

- Better compared with what?
- Increasing compared against what?
- Best with respect to what?
- Ideal compared with whom?

■ Mind reading

This pattern is about assuming that you know what another person is thinking. In one context, let's suppose you are in a meeting, and as you follow the line of discussion you become concerned that a project you were managing is coming under close scrutiny and some criticism. You may begin to have thoughts about the relationship between you and the critics, perhaps one of them is attacking more than the others. It could be the tone of voice, or the body language that you are responding to, and suddenly you find yourself thinking "he's got it in for me."

This is a classic mind read. How do you know he has it in for you? It is more useful in these cases to notice both the verbal and non-verbal cues without attaching meaning. For example:

> He's leaning forward, and his voice has a sharp edge to it com-
> pared to how he usually speaks. He is talking about the problems
> we had in stage two of the project.

Assuming anything further than this is asking for trouble. If your
project is being torn into, you will need your mind's processing
power for rational analysis of the situation, and not waste it on mind
reading what others might be thinking. Of course while you are mind
reading you are deleting lots of other information that could be
useful to you.

Here is another example of mind reading . . .

> I know that you are all wondering who the special guest is going
> to be, but like me, you won't want to miss the important
> announcement which you have all been waiting for.

And the Meta Model responses . . .

- How do you know we are all wondering?
- How do you know I won't want to miss the announcement?
- How do you know we have been waiting for the announcement?

■ Cause and effect

This pattern involves one thing having a causal relationship to
another – A causes B. The problem we create for ourselves with this
pattern is that we are able to construct relationships that create limitations for us.

For example, you could say that "the sun makes the flowers
grow." On the other hand, it is a very different relationship when
you say "the CEO makes me nervous." The former is a biological act
of nature where the sun contributes to the process of photosynthesis
which has a direct biological effect on the flowers. In the latter case,
it is not the CEO that causes nervousness – there is no direct biological link. Flowers cannot *choose* to photosynthesize, but we can
choose our "state" of mind in response to the way we interpret
the world.

In previous chapters you have learned that we are in control of our own minds, so we are able to take responsibility for our own "states." Many people find this concept difficult to grasp, and it can take some time before control is increased over the states of mind and body. Practice is the key, and using the Meta Model on yourself will help you to become more in control. The Meta Model test question for the previous example would be "how exactly does the CEO make you nervous?," or you could say "how do you manage to make yourself nervous when you're with the CEO?"

Here are some more examples:

"If I took a holiday the work would suffer."
"Meetings make me tired."
"Involving the workforce will make many improvements."

And the Meta Model responses . . .

- How would you taking a holiday cause the work to suffer?
- How do you manage to make yourself tired when you're at meetings?
- How will involvement lead to improvements?

■ Complex equivalence

This pattern involves two statements that are given the same meaning. For example, "Your being here means we can start to make progress." *Making progress* is attributed to *your being here*. Here are some more examples . . .

"Arriving late means you have no respect for me."
"These results mean we can relax for a while."
"Being in the top team means we can be proud of ourselves."

And the Meta Model responses . . .

- How does being late mean I have no repect for you?
- How do the results mean that we can relax?
- How does being in the top team mean we can be proud?

■ Presupposition

There are many presuppositional patterns in our language, and some are more useful than others. They are the assumptions we use from day to day that must be true for our language to make sense. For example, "we'll pull out *all* the stops on this campaign" presupposes that on other campaigns not *all* of the stops were pulled out. Here are some more presuppositions . . .

"Are you using Acme Ltd to market the new product?" (Presupposes I am going to market a new product.)

"When you have my experience you'll understand my decision." (Presupposes I don't have your experience and I don't understand your decision.)

"Are you going to pilot the project in the north or the south?" (Presupposes I am going to pilot the project.)

"You have made the same mistake as everyone else." (Presupposes everyone else has made this mistake.)

And the Meta Model responses . . .

- What makes you think I have decided to market the product?
- What makes you think I don't have your experience?
- How do you know I don't understand your decision?
- What leads you to believe I am going to pilot this project?
- How do you know everyone else has made this mistake?

■ Universal quantifiers

These are patterns of generalization and include words like: all, never, every, none, everyone and always. Take "all politicians are untrustworthy." This statement applies a belief about politics to all possible political activities.

Generalizing is a way of extending a statement to cover all possibilities. The tendency is to take one or a number of personal experiences and apply them to all other possibilities. Often these statements are opinions or beliefs, and when we apply these to all possibilities there is a high risk of creating limitations to our thinking process and therefore limiting our flexibility. Here are some examples . . .

"We all must increase our productivity."

"Sales have taken a fall this year."

"Managers don't understand us."

"I can't get people to co-operate with me."

"Property is too expensive in this area."

And the Meta Model responses . . .

- *All*?
- Have *all* sales taken a fall?
- Has *one* manager ever understood you?
- Isn't there *one* person who will co-operate?
- All property?

■ Generalizations

In addition to the universal quantifiers there are a host of other generalizations. Many words used in business are just generalizations of an idea or concept. The most over-used and abused of these is the word "quality." Try asking people at work what quality means and they will probably come up with statements they have learned like "getting it right first time" or "signing your work with excellence." One of the commonest requests I get is to train people in "how to provide a quality service," and I never cease to be amazed at the blank faces I get in response to my first question back to them "and what specifically do your people need to learn to be able to provide a quality service?"

A typical answer to this comes in the form of further generalizations such as "they need better communication skills". Generalizations are useful for global communication. However, the corporate speak of mission statements and quality messages must be translated into language that people can operationalize into their tasks otherwise they are just empty, useless, words.

■ Modal operators of necessity

From early childhood we are conditioned to conform to rules. I remember from my own first months at infant school being told where I *must* and *mustn't* go; where I *ought to* be at certain times;

what I *had to* say when addressing teachers; what I *should* and *shouldn't* do when in the playground. And this conditioning stays with us throughout our lives. We create order in our environment by imposing rules and procedures on ourselves and on others, and sometimes the language we choose to build our own rule structures and moral codes of behavior puts restrictions on our flexibility.

The modal operators we choose also have an influence on our motivation. Someone who thinks "I must complete the order today" is more likely to get the job done than a person who thinks "I might get this order completed today." This has no bearing however on how well the job is done. The first person is likely to stay at work longer than the second in order to finish the task

If you are finding it difficult to motivate yourself to do something, check out the modal operators you are using. A shift from *might* through *must* to *will* can make a big difference especially when you also use the submodalities of *will* from some other task in which you are highly motivated. Use this with the sixth strategy state (chapter 4) to add even more power to your state of motivation.

Modal operators of necessity usually contain the words "ought/ought not, should/shouldn't, must/mustn't, i.e.: I mustn't be late finishing this report." The Meta Model response to a Modal operator of necessity is simply "what would happen if you (did/didn't)/(were/were not)?"

■ Modal operator of possibility

These patterns determine the boundaries of what is possible and impossible for us. In chapter 1, the first two responses to the square peg in the round hole problem contained modal operators of possibility – "I *can't* do that" and "Yes I *can* do that." We set a great many limitations for ourselves with these simple words. I'm not suggesting that we can do anything we wish – some things are physically impossible because of the laws of nature, such as walking on water. However, much potential remains suppressed because of limiting beliefs, and you can notice these through language and the choice of modal operators.

Any time you find yourself using the word "can't," ask yourself if it is a physical limitation, or whether the words "won't" or "haven't learned yet" are more appropriate. As I mentioned in chapter 1, "can't" is a disempowering word. Here are some examples of this pattern . . .

"I can't manage this workload."
"We mustn't upset the applecart."
"It's impossible to get through to him."
"They can't see my argument at all."

And the Meta Model responses are . . .

- What prevents you from managing it?
- What would happen if you did upset it?
- What stops you from getting through?
- What prevents them from seeing it?

Milton Model language contains many more subtleties than I have so far mentioned in this chapter. Developing rapport, pacing and leading, influencing, and offering more behavioral choices are ways of using it, and in the following two chapters I will introduce you to some practical applications of all these uses.

To end this section on Milton Model and Meta Model, here's a letter to a leisure company from Margaret Thatcher when she was Prime Minister of Britain in 1988. Have a go at identifying the Milton Model language, and apply the appropriate Meta Model responses. Have fun.

"This nation's people are its most precious resource. Our companies and organizations, of whatever size and in whatever business, must recognize the need to invest in people to give them the skills of the future. Effective investment in training is crucial to business success. That is why it is so important for employers to be involved in local training provision. Only in this way will we remain competitive and prepared for the challenges ahead.

"Your success in winning a National Training Award is a clear demonstration of your commitment to sound investment in training. I congratulate you. It is vital that others in British industry and commerce should learn from your example."

The language patterns of Milton Model and Meta Model can be used in a variety of ways. There are no strict rules for when you should or should not use a particular pattern. It all depends on the outcome you want to achieve, your intention and your higher purpose. There will be times when artfully vague language will move you towards your outcome, and times when the precision of the Meta Model is the best tool. However you decide to use these tools, take notice of the following health warning.

Using both types of language to excess will result in a severe breakdown of rapport. There is little else in this life so infuriating as someone who perpetually bombards you with the latest technique learned from a training course, and the Meta Model can have a particularly devastating effect. Practice these patterns with yourself as a continual challenge to your autopilot, and apply a high degree of subtlety when using them with other people. And you can use your own words – whatever you are most comfortable with – it's your outcome that is important.

Information frames

Frames are like aspects. If I look out of the front window of my house I get an aspect of the street. If I look out of the back window I get an aspect of the garden and trees beyond. From an upstairs window I get a wider aspect with more content but less detail.

Information frames are useful for thinking from different aspects. I will introduce you to six frames which I have found to be most useful, although there really is no limitation on the frames which you could design for a particular context.

You can use information frames either to clarify and focus your own thinking or the thinking of a group, a client or an employee. Figure 8.3 shows six different frames.

■ Ecology frame

The notion of ecology was first introduced in the section on Well Formed Outcomes and PRI(Ecology)ST. It is useful to switch to this frame when you sense there are ecological issues around that are being overlooked. Some questions to ask from within this frame would be:

- What other consequences could there be if we make this decision?
- How will this decision affect the wider system it is part of?
- Who else should we involve in this decision?

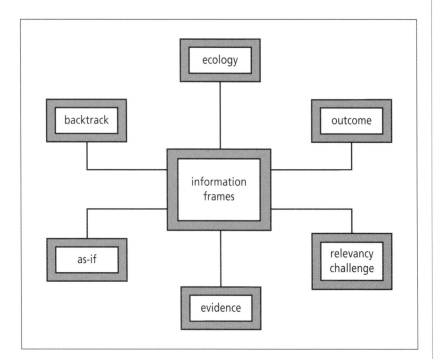

■ FIGURE 8.3
Information frames

NLP is often referred to as "the study of consequences" and the ecology frame ensures that all consequences of an intention are considered. If you are ever responsible for managing a large change project I can think of no better tool to recommend. Sometimes you may get an unsettling feeling about a decision with no real evidence to back up a postponement. This is your incongruency signal cutting in and warning you that something has been overlooked. A switch to the ecology frame could avoid a potential future blunder.

■ Outcome frame

Outcomes were covered in detail in chapter 3. The purpose of this frame is to keep thinking focussed on agreed aims while considering other possible outcomes. It is often necessary to remind people of outcomes when activity begins to wander off track.

■ Relevancy challenge frame

At times it is important to keep full concentration on achieving an outcome, and you may sense a comment or an action that takes you off track. The relevancy challenge frame is similar to the outcome frame in that its purpose is to maintain focus. The relevancy challenge would be used in an immediate way as soon as a deviation was sensed. Practice this with your own thinking when it is important to keep focussed for an extended period of time. Questions to ask are:

- How does this/that help achieve the outcome?
- What relevance does this/that have to the outcome?

■ Evidence frame

Sometimes you may find yourself, or your group, arriving at decisions without sufficient reason for doing so. In these situations the evidence frame will clarify your purpose and intention. This is a useful frame for quality improvement groups and problem solvers in general who need evidence with which to make comparisons between current and desired states. You will find the evidence frame useful for testing your own assumptions and actions. Are you operating towards achieving an outcome that has measurable evidence criteria? What evidence is there to determine how far you are from your outcomes?

■ As-if frame

The purpose of the "as-if" frame is to stimulate creativity. It was used in the "building success into future events" exercise in chapter 5 where you were invited to imagine a future event as-if it were happening now. This is a useful frame to check out reasons for incongruence signals, particularly where you have major personal decisions to make like job moves, additional roles or company moves. Visualizing yourself as-if you have made the change by running the movie through in your mind will help to highlight the part of the change that is generating the incongruence signal.

As-if frames are ideal for creativity workshops and scenario planning sessions. The question to ask is "what would happen if . . .?

■ Backtrack frame

This frame is used to clarify understanding of previous information before proceeding further. It is used to deepen rapport through reflection of the words, tonalities and gestures used by others (these points will be covered in greater detail in the next chapter). It is also useful as a coaching tool to enhance the thinking of others.

For example, consider a coaching session where the outcome is to develop problem solving abilities while working on a performance objective . . .

> Manager: *"Tell me where you are on the (x) project."*
>
> Employee: *"I'm ready to approach the project board for an agreement to begin stage two."*
>
> Manager: *"What do you need to do in order to achieve that?"* (backtrack)
>
> Employee: *"Send them a detailed and costed plan."*
>
> Manager: *"That's right – and what will you need to produce the plan?"* (backtrack).
>
> Employee: *"I'll need resource allocation reports from engineering, and up-to-date costs for materials and labour."*
>
> Manager: *"How do you propose to go about getting them?"* (backtrack) *etc . . . etc . . . etc.*

Reframing

To reframe is to change the meaning about something which causes a change in perception and attitude and opens up new possibilities. This is a powerful technique for which there are many examples in everyday business life – for example: the meeting with an unsettling authoritarian could mean that "you interact from a defensive position with safety and survival in mind." Reframed to mean "a challenge to discover how much you can influence the person toward your ideas" would put you in a more resourceful state and would certainly influence your behavior and therefore also the outcome of the meeting.

A keynote speaker late for an important business conference walked onto the stage 45 minutes late and said "it's not that I'm late – I'm here as a result of foresight – you see my scheduled flight was delayed four hours, but luckily I decided to drive so that I could give my very sick neighbour a lift to the hospital. Had I taken my scheduled flight I would not be here at all, and perhaps neither would my neighbour. Thank you for your patience . . ."

Many business problems are divergent by nature, which can cause managers to suffer from the symptoms of stress. To quote Albert Einstein "in the middle of difficulty lies opportunity" offers these managers a superb reframe for divergent problem situations. Working with opportunities is much more rewarding than working with problems – and the attitude is much healthier also.

I have found enormous interest in reframing from my management students. It is often seen as a quick remedy for negativity and cynicism. In chapter 6 you were introduced to a number of reframing examples, one of which was a reframe around the meaning of work. In one of my workshops we were dealing with the meaning of cynicism with a small group of managers who had been with the company for a reasonably long period. Their problem was that *they had seen and heard it all before. It didn't work last time and it won't work this time. They're making decisions in the dark.* These were some of the phrases they were using.

They were not in a resourceful state for learning and they agreed it was because they were cynical about any change which top management introduced. I could have chosen to work with their meaning of work, but it was much easier working with their meaning of cynicism. I first got them all to agree that cynicism meant: *they had seen it all before and showed little confidence in top management.* I then used a *higher chunk* within an *evidence frame* and a change of *perceptual position* to unsettle this meaning by saying: "if you have little confidence in our top team, who by the way have demonstrated their ability to grow a successful company (higher chunk) which pays our wages and expenses every month (evidence), then who can you put your confidence in?" This rattled them as I continued with "And just imagine how the top team might interpret your cynicism (second perceptual position). What words do you think they might come up with for how you are reacting to their plans?"

This did it. You could see the change taking place as they were knocked back, almost speechless. For the remainder of the workshop they were quite positive and began to discuss problems rationally with each other. The change of meaning about their cynical attitude helped them to realize how unproductive they had been – knocking top management rather than dealing with the problems.

Metaphor

Prince Llewelyn lived in a castle in Wales. One day the Prince went out leaving his faithful and trusting dog Gelert to watch over his young son and protect him from wolves which roamed freely in the nearby forest. When the prince returned to the castle he found to his horror that his son was missing from his cradle which had been upturned. There were bloodstains around the cradle and on the floor. He turned to find Gelert who was panting heavily with blood around his mouth. Distressed and fearing the worst, the prince drew his sword and stabbed Gelert through the heart. The prince's head dropped and his heart sank at what had happened, then from behind a curtain he heard a cry. It was his son, alive and well, standing next to the dead body of a wolf.

One of the earliest forms of learning and still the most impactful is the metaphor. This (true) story of Gelert the faithful dog can be used to teach the consequences of jumping to conclusions. The right metaphor, when told in an appropriate context, can deliver an extremely powerful learning message to the unconscious mind. Metaphors are memorable, and can contain emotions as well as learning. Humor is ideally suited to metaphor. A great metaphor delivered well can lead an audience through many emotional states, from humor to heartbreak.

The story of the Prince and Gelert has a cautionary message – a "*moving away from* making wrong decisions." This may be what is required for a particular purpose, and you would need some methodology for designing a positive direction for the listener to *move towards* also.

Speak clearly, if you
speak at all;
Carve every word
before you let it fall.

DR OLIVER WENDELL
HOLMES (1809–94)
American writer and
physician

Congruence

The notion of congruence has been dealt with a number of times already in previous chapters. It is something that, like ecology, winds and twists around every element of NLP. It is important to cover congruence in the context of language because of the huge impact it can have on organizational effectiveness.

Mistrust is often the cause of incongruence which leads to decreased performance. A big problem here is that many people don't seem to recognize when they are being incongruent. Yet other people pick up these signals unconsciously and respond accordingly. The director who sends all his managers on coaching and mentoring training, and yet who continues to communicate in a dictatorial way will transmit strong signals of incongruence between what he says and what he does.

Congruence requires a manager to become a paragon for others to follow. The old statements of leadership apply – lead by example, set standards for others, be a role model for others. If you are incongruent in your communication, then expect puzzling behavior and low levels of creativity from your employees. If you are congruent, accept the respect others will give to you.

INFLUENCE AND PERSUASION

■ **Trust**

■ **Like me – like you**

■ **A communication process – the TOTE model**

■ **Rapport**

■ **Sensory information**

■ **Pacing**

■ **Leading**

■ **Anchoring**

Sensory acuity / Calibration / Matching and mirroring / Pacing
values / Example scenario 1 – The negotiation /
Example scenario 2 – The inquest

Business runs on decisions and interactions between people. From strategic decisions made by the board of directors to the everyday decisions of managers and employees, the well-being of any organization depends upon the quality of interaction and decision-making. You have certain responsibilities to carry out as a manager and your responsibilities rely upon specific business and personal objectives being achieved.

As work environments become less structured, and contribution replaces status as a personal profile rating, the command and control style of managing is quickly becoming redundant. The time when a manager could use rank to ensure compliance with his wishes is almost gone. Nowadays compliance is a rusting management tool – best left with law and order enforcement agencies. Thankfully compliance is fast being replaced by more humane strategies of involvement and participation. Alongside this change in management style you have a change in influencing methods.

The science of influencing has evolved through two stages, the first being authoritative compliance, and the second being assertiveness skills. To be congruent with an empowering management style, influencing in the modern organization now requires a third stage – the more subtle approach offered by NLP.

To belong to an organization and have no influence over its operations is to be subservient to the ideas of others. "Yes men" are like this – docile, passive, and compliant. Business today needs fewer "yes men" and more creative people who are prepared to take risks, try new angles, and stretch the horizons of possibility. To do this requires a questioning mind, a passion for difference and change, and an ability to align others behind your thinking.

Yet curiosity and passion alone are wasted if you are unable to generate interest from others in the organization. It is no use having the best idea since sliced bread if you are unable to persuade others to buy it. Galileo was a brilliant scientist whose curious mind led him to discover that, contrary to the beliefs of the Catholic church in the 17th century, the Earth was not an unmoving mass at the centre of the universe. Sadly, Galileo did not have the ability to influence his contemporaries and his published work "dialog on two world systems" led him to being placed under house arrest for the remainder of his life.

It is no use having the best idea since sliced bread if you are unable to persuade others to buy it.

To influence requires a respect for the other person's model of the world. It also needs integrity, patience and understanding. Without these qualities your attempts to influence others may be perceived as manipulative, in which case your proposals are likely to fall on deaf ears. This brings us back to intention and purpose. If you have a worthwhile purpose with well formed outcomes, and if your intention is biased toward the business and not toward political gain, then you have the necessary basic principles for influencing *respectfully*.

To influence requires a respect for the other person's model of the world.

Trust

People will allow themselves to be influenced by people they trust. The opposite is also true. Have you ever made a major purchase from someone you didn't trust? I doubt it. In fact when faced with a choice, most people would rather buy a product which just falls short of meeting their needs from someone they trust, than buy an ideal product from someone they don't.

Having integrity of purpose and intentions will be rewarded with trust, yet this is not enough. There is a capability you can develop which is equally as fundamental and important as trust – "being liked." It is possible to trust someone and to dislike them, although trusting and liking are often closely linked. Do you have friends that you don't trust to return items you have loaned them? If a person *trusts* you and *likes* you, the basic requisites for influence are established.

Having integrity of purpose and intentions will be rewarded with trust.

Like me – like you

A very good friend of mine has a great ability to be like the person or group he is with. I have observed him discussing strategy with CEOs, swapping gossip with the cleaning lady, telling dirty jokes to engineers, and engaging a Chinese chef in the culinary subtleties of Cantonese speciality dishes. Like a chameleon that changes color to blend in with its environment, he has the behavioral flexibility to blend in with whoever he is interacting with.

People like people who are like them, and they are cautious of people who are not like them. The more you are like someone, the better understanding you will have of their model of the world. It's a dynamic on which all people base their social activities and relationships around – it is deep rooted in our psyche. Liking and trusting can be left to happen naturally, or you can have the behavioral flexibility to generate liking and trust with intention and purpose.

A communication process – the TOTE model

[1] G Miller, E Galanter, K Pribram, *Plans and the Structure of Behaviour*, Holt, Rinehart and Winston; 1960.

You were introduced to a modified version of the tote model[1] in chapter 1 where I explained how capabilities are a function of distinctions and a continual comparison against a pre-defined goal. My intention in using figure 1.3 was to show the relationship between a number of elements in the development of capabilities. Figure 9.1 shows a simplified version of the tote model which can be adapted for any human communication process.

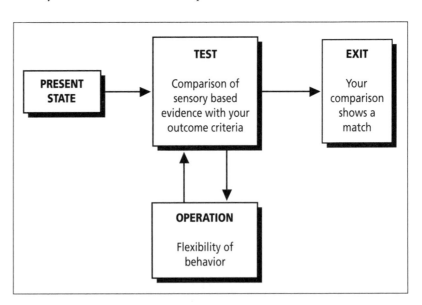

■ FIGURE 9.1
The TOTE model

TOTE is a mnemonic for "Test – Operate – Test – Exit" that provides a feedback loop for comparing where you are (present state) with where you want to be (your outcome). The Test is a comparison of what sensory-based evidence you have against what you have previously defined in your outcome. If you get a mismatch then you loop back through the Operation and do something else. If what you are doing isn't working – do something different. You Test again, and keep going around this loop until you get a match. Then you can Exit the TOTE.

Thinking about the communication process in TOTES emphasizes the need to be flexible. All communication can be defined as a series of nested TOTES where your outcome on one level might be to educate other people in a new procedure, and on another to build rapport with one manager so that they are more susceptible to accepting your new procedure. In either case, whether your outcome is on a macro or micro level, the process is exactly the same. And within any TOTE there are some processes for really *connecting* with people, and increasing your capability to be flexible.

NLP

If what you are doing isn't working – do something different.

Rapport

Building rapport with people in your organization is one of the most productive activities you can engage in. Having a good rapport with people makes everything so much easier. If one of your outcomes requires the influence of a certain person, then I can think of nothing more outcome-oriented than rapport building with this person, even if it means going out of your way to find an opportunity to do so. In the same way that trust and liking can be generated intentionally, so can rapport.

Yet rapport is much more than gaining trust and getting people to like you – it is being like them. Rapport is about sameness, and the flexibility to be the same as others requires the qualities of a chameleon – to be like whoever you want to be for the purpose of building rapport. In any interaction, whenever you encounter resistance, it is a sign of a lack of rapport. Before I continue with the components of rapport, there are some key skills to master.

NLP

In any interaction, whenever you encounter resistance, it is a sign of a lack of rapport.

Sensory information

Referring to the TOTE model, your outcomes will contain sensory based evidence to ascertain how close you are to achieving them. You have learned how a person's behavior provides cues to their thought processes, and you know that there is much more meaning under the surface of the words a person uses than is immediately apparent. Remember also that 55 percent of someone's message is contained in their physiology and 38 percent in their vocal qualities. Aside from the words a person uses there is an enormous amount of information available that is vital in understanding a person, gaining their trust, building rapport and having an influence on them.

■ Sensory acuity

Gathering sensory information requires practice – and the act of practicing is itself a rapport-building activity. You are showing interest in people, and most people enjoy the experience of talking with someone who is interested in them. When you are being receptive to sensory information you need to have your attention focussed entirely outside – this is called being in "uptime" – totally alert with all your sensory receptors watching, listening, smelling, tasting and feeling the changes going on in the world around you. Being in "downtime" is the opposite of this where your attention is directed inside as you engage in reflective visualization, internal dialog or feeling. Whenever you are in downtime you are missing sensory evidence from the outside world.

Sensory acuity requires high states of uptime. As most people have preferences over the use of their senses, the strongest being the primary modality, it is a good idea to begin developing the senses which you use least of all. After much practice your sensory acuity will become sharper.

It is often the most subtle changes that give the most significant cues to a person's thought process. The late British poet Siegfried Sassoon once said "in me the tiger sniffs the rose" which is an excellent metaphor for sensory acuity. Recently I asked a consultant to take responsibility for one of my own training programs. After discussing the implications she said "OK, I'm comfortable with that" – but I picked up a slight wavering in her voice that was incongruent with her words. It was difficult for me to begin interrogating her so I just said "actually it's not fair of me to foist this onto you just now – there are some loose ends which I should tidy up first."

I didn't know what the incongruency was about (and I don't think she was fully aware of it at the time), but sure enough about three weeks later I learned that her knowledge of the program was very thin and she thanked me for retracting the responsibility. She initially accepted responsibility for the program for the wrong reason. If you have ever persuaded someone to do something they don't like doing, you are likely to have noticed a signal of incongruence from some part of their neurology. The words can say "yes" while, at the same time, the unconscious is saying "no." The most important information about a person is their behavior.

■ Calibration

This is the term given to the act of recognizing state changes in others and noticing specific conditions of posture, breathing, skin tone, expression, voice qualities etc. We need to be in uptime exercising our sensory acuity to notice the subtle changes in a person's state. As long as we exist and have form we also will have a *state* which is continually changing. It is easy to notice a change from smiling to crying – that doesn't take a tremendous amount of sensory acuity, but many cues are more subtle than this.

Calibration is noticing exactly what you sense and nothing more. For example, you may be in a meeting and notice the chairman looking at you with a tightened forehead, reddish skin, fast breathing and with his fists clenched on the table. This is calibration. On the other hand you might notice these things and think "he's upset about something – he's going to have a dig at me." This is mind reading. Later in this chapter I will give you some examples of state calibration.

Pacing

If you were to sit outside on the sidewalk in a large town and watch people as they passed by, you would notice many differences between them. If I asked you to notice the speed at which their neurology is working, watching their walking pace, stride, breathing rate, facial expressions, eye movements, gestures, and draw graphs

NLP

The most important information about a person is their behavior.

to represent the differences, you would end up with a range of graphs between two extremes (refer to figure 9.2).

Now, imagine putting together two people from each extreme. How would you describe their communication? Rapport would be out of the question while they are in such different neurological states from each other. For rapport to happen they will need to get rhythmically closer to each other.

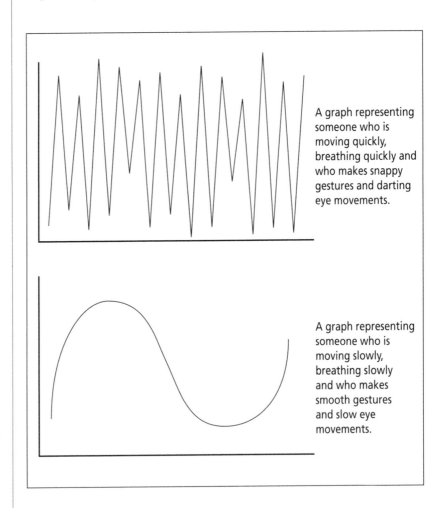

A graph representing someone who is moving quickly, breathing quickly and who makes snappy gestures and darting eye movements.

A graph representing someone who is moving slowly, breathing slowly and who makes smooth gestures and slow eye movements.

■ FIGURE 9.2
Extreme
neurological states

Rapport can be developed by pacing various physical and mental conditions. To pace someone's breathing is very powerful because of the link to the visual, auditory and kinesthetic modalities (refer to chapter 7). You can also pace body language by matching and mirroring.

■ Matching and mirroring

If you have ever watched people who have deep rapport with one another you will notice how closely their body posture, gestures and voice qualities are matched. Notice two lovers in a restaurant, or two people drinking at a bar, or a group of managers at a meeting. Matching is an unconscious form of communication that bonds relationships by deepening rapport. Matching is doing the same, i.e. sitting directly opposite someone you match a lean to the right with a lean to your right. Mirroring is where you match their left with your right as a mirror image. You can be subtle about this. If you match the other person too precisely it can be noticed at the conscious level in which case you may be accused of mimicking.

The intention of matching and mirroring is to communicate with the unconscious mind by getting into the same "state" as the other person. Matching physiology is the simplest way of doing this. It is almost impossible to get into a state of high self-confidence when your body is drooping, your head is hung low, face muscles relaxed, and your eyes looking down. Try it for yourself, then do the opposite – body upright, head up, and eyes up – now smile . . . and notice the difference in your state!

When you are matching gestures do so when it is your turn to speak, rather than when the other person is gesturing. A hunch of the shoulders, a hand on the breast, an open hand, a pointing finger – these are all unconscious communication signals which you can match or mirror. When matching the voice, listen for rhythm, volume, speed, tone and pitch. Fast talkers (strong visual people) are quickly frustrated by slow talkers (strong kinesthetics) and slow talkers often find fast talkers difficult to follow. Visual people can slow their speech down by breathing more slowly deep in the stomach area, and kinesthetic people can speed up their rate of speech by increasing their rate of breathing and moving it to the higher chest area.

Notice also the sensory predicates people use. If you wanted to *break* rapport with someone who says to you "we had a rough ride getting to grips with the alpha project thanks to the project team," reply with "I can imagine what a dim view you must have of them." When you use predicates from a person's preferred sensory system

Matching is an unconscious form of communication that bonds relationships by deepening rapport.

you are easier to listen to and understand. Build a vocabulary of predicates and practice matching. In a safe environment, mismatch a person's predicates and notice the response you get compared to when you are matching.

■ Pacing values

Anyone who has worked overseas in different cultures will realize the importance of values. In Arab countries it is not unusual to arrive for a meeting and have to wait hours or even days with other guests before you are entertained. The more values you can pace, the closer you will get to the person you are communicating with, and the deeper your rapport will be. Here is a list of contexts to help you notice values.

Cultural values

These could be the values of a nation's culture as in the Arab example, or an organizational culture. I have noticed that some companies are introducing a "casual clothes" day for their employees. Some people think that the classic business suit is an unnecessary item while others claim it projects a professional and orderly aspect of your character. When suited client meets casual supplier you get a cultural mismatch.

Organizational values

These are not so much cultural human rituals like the wearing of suits, they are more intrinsic to the business operation. Sales executives know these values extremely well. You can find them in reception halls and executive meeting rooms; framed certificates for "commitment to quality" and engraved plaques for "service to the community" or "service to the environment." Whatever product you want to sell a company, make sure it contributes to the company's values. Other values of this type which you may come across are "innovation," "market leaders," "preferred partners," "the biggest and best," and "investor in people." These values are often the key to successful sales campaigns and negotiations. Mismatching an organization's values is probably the quickest way of losing rapport and business.

Group values

At a group level in any organization you can come across many different value systems operating at the same time. Groups that co-exist in the same building can have widely differing values. A production team may have values around team working and efficiency while an R&D group might espouse the importance of being innovative. If you wanted to influence me you would need to pace my group values around responsibility, autonomy and efficiency.

Do you recall the experience I shared with you (chapter 1) of returning from a course where I learned the structure for effective meetings? The tutor neglected to warn me about values, and upon returning from the course I mismatched the values of a management group by cutting through their social chatter with a structural comment.

Role values

People attach certain importance to their roles. This is the reason why a person chooses a particular role for themselves, and values may be vastly different across roles. You may recall, in chapter 1, how changing a role label also changed the perception and meaning of that role – from "information manager" to "educator" for example. For the past three years I have been entertained by a whole bunch of sales and marketing people, from the same company, desperate for the business I can put their way. Their approach is always the same, telling me they are the biggest and best and they are going to get my business. Their role values are around "key result areas," "profit," and "growth." My role values are concerned with logistics and effectiveness of training investment. And what makes me smile the most is that I have told them this and yet they persist in mismatching my values and widening the gulf between us.

Personal values

The range here is almost limitless, encompassing values concerned with family, finance, intellect, relationships, work style, enjoyment, leisure, socializing, hobbies, interests, and sport. These values are often exposed in casual conversation, as you are waiting for a meeting to start or over lunch. Stay with these conversations for a while

– at least until you have done some pacing. These values also present themselves as elements of a person's home and office environment – the golfing trophy, the club tie, the car sticker, the family photograph, the key fob etc, etc. These material accessories are extensions to our personality and of real importance to us.

Values are hierarchical and vary in strength. Chapter 1 explored how "means" values are linked to higher level "end" values. The same is true for group values and personal values. In almost every case, when a choice must be made, group values will override personal values, although most people will join groups that have similar values to their own.

Values are hierarchical and vary in strength.

Leading

Pacing will build rapport, gain trust and portray a likeable personality. Once you have mastered the art of pacing you can begin to influence people by leading them in the direction you want them to go. Some people are natural leaders and will hold a focal point while others seem content to follow. Your skill at pacing will put you in this same position, where others are content to follow you because they trust and like you. Of course your proposals have to be sound – don't expect people to follow your lead if you are offering inappropriate plans.

The key to pacing and leading is a seamless transition. You can simply test whether you have paced sufficiently by adjusting your body posture and noticing if the other person/people follow you. If they do, you can continue to lead. If not, you need more rapport. I want to go through some practical scenarios explaining how you might use pacing and leading, but first there is one more technique for your toolbag.

Anchoring

There is a story about a soldier who, years after serving in Vietnam, would throw himself to the ground upon hearing a car backfire. This physiological reaction had been "anchored" to the sound of gunfire from the countless number of times he avoided the real thing in Vietnam. Many of our memories are anchored to external stimuli. The sound of a ringing bell can take you right back to your school-days. The smell of cod liver oil reminds me of my pre-school days where a pill a day was compulsory.

The external stimulus triggers an emotional state accessed from memory. Some of our anchors access pleasant emotions while others access unpleasant ones. Knowing about anchors, and how the process of anchoring works, we are able to use them to our advantage. We all unconsciously anchor states in each other every day. I know of one manager who is very intelligent, experienced, and professional in his role, and yet his boss, the managing director, has managed to anchor a state of subservience (my label) which is triggered by the sound of his voice. I have observed this state change from his conversations with the MD over the telephone as well as face-to-face. There is a complete physiological shift from "upright with head slightly down" to "bent forward and hunched with the head slightly back."

This is an example of an auditory anchor. A visual anchor might be a facial expression, a photograph or a picture. A kinesthetic anchor might be a pat on the back or a squeeze of the hand. There are times when you may want to use some "feeling good" anchors, at other times you may want to access states of "creativity," "critical analysis," or "intense concentration." How about anchoring your sixth strategy state to make it instantly accessible any time you want it? You can anchor states of resourcefulness for yourself, and I will be explaining how to do this in chapter 10 – Influencing the masses, when we take a look at the corporate large group presentation.

You can set anchors in any modality – visual, auditory, kinesthetic, olfactory or gustatory. The two latter are not so useful in business. The process for setting an anchor is simple:

1 Calibrate the state you want to anchor.
2 Anchor the state with a unique stimulus (V, A, K or any combination).
3 Change the state of the subject being calibrated.
4 Fire your anchor (apply the same unique stimulus as in 2 above) and calibrate again for the state change you want.

The key to successful anchoring is:

1 Uniqueness of the stimulus. Combinations of voice tone, gesture, and visuals work well. If you catch someone in an intense state of agreement you might anchor this by standing tall, raising your voice tone, pointing upward with your hand and saying "It's good to have agreements." At some later stage when you want an agreement, run exactly the same stimulus to access the agreement state as you make the proposal. Kinesthetic anchoring is powerful, but in some business contexts touching others may break rapport.

2 Timing States vary in intensity usually rising to a peak then falling off. Sometimes the rise and fall may be so fast that you miss it. This is where your sensory acuity comes in. You want to set your anchor just before the state peaks (refer to figure 9.3). Low intensity states are not worth anchoring as they will not have the effect you desire. Anchor states that are worth accessing again. Here are some examples of states that might be worth accessing in others – agreement, enjoyment, concentration, creativity, relaxation, attentive, learning.

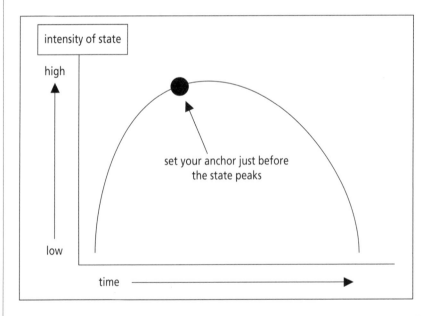

■ FIGURE 9.3
Applying an anchor
– timing

3 Easy to repeat You may want to set an anchor more than once, so make your anchors easy to remember and repeat. Remember it has to be unique, and when you use it you have to repeat exactly what you did when you first set it up. Standing on your head and singing may be unique, but how easy is it to repeat?

The following examples include some of the techniques covered so far in this section with one or two additional techniques.

■ Example scenario 1: The negotiation

George is a manager negotiating with a supplier (Laura) in the final stage of a tender to place a $10 million computer supply contract. George's outcome is to get Laura to drop her price to $7.5 million because she represents the preferred supplier whose bid price of $10 million is way too high. Laura's outcome is to secure this contract for no less than 15 percent below the bid price ($8.5 million). Laura is pacing and leading George.

George: "Hello Laura, it's good to see you again. How are you?"
Laura: "I'm fine, how are you George?"
George: "I'm digging around for cost savings I'm afraid."
Laura: "That feels familiar. I'm uncomfortable with my household bills at the moment, I've simply got to tighten up somehow."

(Matching kinesthetic predicates, the value of making cost savings, breathing, posture, and voice qualities.)

George: "Well, let's get down to business. I am drawn to your proposal, and it went down well with the quality manager – but I must admit the overall cost shocked us both."
Laura: "You know that we have never held back on quality before. It will always play a leading role in our service delivery. I am keen to explore how we can remove the shock – tell me, what would get you to feel more at ease with the proposal?"

(Pacing the past and future, matching kinesthetic predicates, breathing, and voice qualities. There is also an embedded suggestion "we can remove the shock" which is marked out using a lower voice tone. Laura ends by asking a question with the purpose of accessing a "feel good" state which she will attempt to anchor.)

George: "Cut the price by 50 percent and invoice in arrears?" This is a half-serious answer made with a light-hearted laugh which is turned into a question by a higher voice tone at the end.

Laura: "I like clients with a sense of humor like you George. How would you feel if I were to cut the cost by say 12.5 percent which I could do by reducing part of the service?"

(The words "I like" were emphasized by volume and tone at the same time as she tapped her fingers sharply on the desk – this combination set up a unique auditory stimulus anchor for George's light-hearted laugh. More value matching at the personal level (sense of humour) with the initial sentence.)

George: "That's moving in the right direction, but I was hoping for more than 12.5 percent; can you move any further?"

(George is persistent but happy to be led by Laura because the rapport is so good. He is enjoying himself.)

Laura: "I can move a little further, I have always managed to accommodate you in the past, haven't I? I will have to review the services though. Let me recap for a moment. I know you do not expect me to compromise on quality, and yet you want a reduction in excess of 12.5 percent. I could revise the service offering to reduce our costs, but that would be a compromise on the service to your customers. I feel sure that, like me, you would rather compromise on the price than on quality or service (fires anchor). I am happy to offer you 14 percent right now on the proposal as it stands with no compromise on quality and service. Can we strike a deal on this now?"

(More matching and pacing. Leading begins when she starts to recap. Lots of matching values – quality and service. More rapport building with the words "I feel sure that, like me" which contains an embedded suggestion "like me." The question "haven't I" is tagged on to the end of a sentence intentionally to get George to say the word "yes" which is an agreement state. Laura fires her anchor by using the same voice tone that was used to set the anchor as she taps the table in the same place to make the same sound. The anchor is fired to access George's light-hearted laugh state, just as she begins to make her final offer.)

■ Example scenario 2: The inquest

Jeff is a service manager being called to explain a major service incident by his client, Mike, whose outcome is to give Jeff a hard time and keep him in an underdog position. Jeff's outcome is to use the meeting as an opportunity to build rapport and strengthen their relationship. Jeff is pacing and leading Mike.

Mike: "Hello Jeff, sit down. Coffee?"

Jeff: "Yes please".

Mike: "I have to say that this incident is possibly the worst on record and I will need a complete account of what happened. I also want to be assured that you are capable of preventing any future occurrence."

Jeff: "The incident has been clearly documented in this report. You'll find it contains complete details of what happened which I will be happy to discuss with you."

(Jeff has avoided taking a defensive position, given Mark what he asked for, and paced his auditory predicates, breathing, posture, and voice qualities.)

Mike: "What do you have to say to reassure me, and my colleagues, that your organization is capable of supplying us with a consistent service that complies with our standards?"

Jeff: "We have always listened consistently to your needs, and complied with your requests for additional services. I want to state my concern over this one incident, and at the same time assure you, and your colleagues, that we will remain tuned in to the standards written in the service criteria which were established when we first signed the contract."

(Pacing values of consistency and standards, chunking up from the incident to "service criteria," matching predicates, breathing, posture, and voice qualities.)

Mike: "Well, that's true, perhaps this incident was caused by human error, in which case there is still no excuse for what happened."

Jeff: "The report clearly explains the cause. But you know, this is one of only five problems – this year. On a contract of this size I am not too concerned at our overall performance which, as you agreed, is meeting the overall service criteria. We have achieved this position by listening and articulating our operation, consistently meeting your evolving standards. This incident has been taken seriously, as you will tell from the detail in the report, and we are already writing new procedures from what we have learned."

(More matching of predicates and pacing of values. Jeff begins to pace the conversation here as he slowly changes his posture, voice tones, and gestures to strengthen his words which have moved focus from the incident to higher level values, achievement, procedures, and learning.)

Pacing an organization needs to be done on many different levels all at the same time.

In extreme examples where someone is really against you, patience is the key. Just keep matching, mirroring, and pacing the whole neurology and you will eventually get rapport to a level at which you can begin to lead. Pacing an organization needs to be done on many different levels all at the same time. Dave Sibley, a top sales executive in the computer industry, has just secured the biggest desktop computing contract in Europe – British Telecom. It is worth over £60 million per year. His strategy was to match and pace values at many different levels in the organization and build rapport. It took him about four years to move from a position of being unknown and uninvited, to having his photograph taken with the director of IT services. That's the power of rapport.

This chapter has introduced you to some powerful techniques for influencing and persuading in many day-to-day situations. The next chapter builds on this theme by inviting you to discover even more techniques. The chosen context in which they are introduced to you is one that all managers must face from time to time – the corporate presentation. This is one of the few activities to strike fear in the hearts of managers – yet with a simple reframe it can be the most opportune moment for influencing the thinking of the masses and leading them to favor your ideas and initiatives – *to actualize a personal competitive advantage!*

INFLUENCING THE MASSES

■ **Purpose, intention, and outcomes**

■ **Content – the material**

■ **Language**

■ **State control**

■ **Connecting with your audience**

■ **Handling questions from the audience**

Producing the material / Connecting with individuals /
Sequencing the material / Humor / Metaphor / Notes / Identity /
Values and beliefs / Pre-framing / Physiology / Voice /
Hypothetical and judgmental questions / Questions or
statements from confused minds / The personal attack / The
direct challenge / Using your body

Let thy speech be short, comprehending much in few words.

<small>APROCRYPHA</small>
Ecclesiasticus

For many managers, the thought of giving a presentation before a large group is one of their biggest fears. It is often considered as an opportunity to blow personal credibility with a lot of people in one go. This fear is responsible for many creative avoidance strategies. The "moving away from" metaprogram can kick-in with full strength at the slightest apprehension of your first presentation.

Yet the corporate presentation is an ideal vehicle for connecting with large numbers of people. It is a chance to build rapport and be influential in a big way. If you are well practiced at speaking to groups you may have already overcome the "fear" barrier, leaving your mind free to discover ways of increasing the impact for your next major presentation. Whatever your experience in addressing large groups, it is a skill which can be learned and improved upon like any other, and I will be using the material covered so far to program a sixth strategy state and help develop your skill in this area.

Purpose, intention, and outcomes

Whenever you get the opportunity to address a group, make the most of it. Consider it a chance to spin your web of influence and rapport across a wider area. You may have been asked by someone else to present some information either to a client, or to an internal group. This will be the "purpose" for the presentation. Whatever the external purpose, as long as it is fulfilled, you may be able to add some of your own personal intentions and outcomes. Ask yourself "what opportunities does this occasion present for me?"

I have split the whole thing into two parts – (1) the content of your presentation covering the material and how to put it together, and (2) the process by which you will deliver it covering the neuro-linguistic interaction between you and your audience. You can use either part to build in some of your own intentions and outcomes like developing rapport and influencing. It is worth asking the event sponsor for extra time to cover your own outcomes. "Muscling in" on other people's events can have big payoffs as long as your audience perceives your pitch as relevant and worthwhile. Just be careful to maintain rapport with the sponsors also.

Consider addressing a group to be a chance to spin your web of influence and rapport across a wider area.

Ask yourself "what opportunities does this occasion present for me?"

Remember that the process part of your presentation will contain 93 percent of your overall message, while the content part is a mere 7 percent (refer chapter 7), so you will be doing much of your rapport building through your physiology and voice qualities. However, the 7 percent content is just as important because this is what your audience will be coming for. I shall cover the content part first.

The process part of your presentation will contain 93 percent of your overall message.

Content – the material

You must know your subject inside out. The worst presentations are often those where the presenter has only a thin knowledge of the subject. You will need all your conscious mindpower for the process part, and for remembering the sequence of the material, so make sure you are absolutely comfortable with the subject you will be presenting. You also need to know something about your audience so that you can pitch your material at the right level. Here are some questions to ask about the audience beforehand.

- Who has set their expectations, and what are they?
- Why do they need to know what you will be telling them?
- What do they already know about your subject?
- What do they need to know?
- What don't they need to know?
- How much detail do they need?
- How will the information be of use to them?

On occasions you may not be able to get the answers to these questions before the presentation. That's OK, you can ask them at the beginning like this:

"Before I begin it would be useful for me to find out how much you know about this subject – please raise your hand if you know nothing at all about this. OK, good. Who has heard of _____ ? I see. And raise your hand if you have experience of _____. Thank you, that gives me a rough idea of where to begin."

As you ask people to raise their hands, raise yours also as a gesture for them to follow. If you don't you could get blank stares. Let them know what you expect of them by pacing and leading at all times.

■ Producing the material

This of course depends on the type of presentation you are giving. If you have purely statistical data you will want to find an interesting way of presenting it. Charts with lots of numbers are fine if you want to send your audience to sleep. It's always a good idea to brainstorm for ideas even if you already have the material at hand. Persuade some colleagues to help you generate ideas, the more people helping – the more ideas you will get. Search for different ways of presenting material, especially data which some people may perceive as boring. Attention levels will be higher, and retention will be greater when you present your information in all of the three main sensory modalities – visual, auditory and kinesthetic.

Use of acting, role play, singing, games, music and brightly colored visuals will make your presentation exciting. Don't be afraid of exaggerating to make a point and to involve people – if you do a good job at pacing people you will be surprised at how far you can lead them into the realms of enjoyment. If you have multi-media facilities make the best use of them to give your audience a full all-round sensory experience.

■ Connecting with individuals

As you begin to gather material, make sure you cover three basic questions your audience will be asking of you.

- Why are you telling us this?
- What are you saying?
- What use is it to me?

Some people need you to answer the question "why" before they will allow themselves to take in your information. They must have a reason for listening, so make sure you have reasons, and that you include them at the beginning of the presentation, e.g.: "you need to know this new policy because, as we begin trading in Europe, each

If you do a good job at pacing people you will be surprised at how far you can lead them into the realms of enjoyment.

transaction will be subject to it and you will lose commission each time you get it wrong. You will also be rewarded with an extra 5 percent each time you get it right."

Other people aren't interested in "why?," they just want you to give them the information in as much detail as possible – these people need to know the answer to the question "what?" Some people want to know "how?" they will be able to use your information. They need to fit it into a context which is real for them. And in every audience you will have a mix of metaprograms. *Global* people will expect to see a big picture. *Detail* people will want the specifics.

Imagine you are presenting a new manufacturing process to a client. You don't want too much detail in the presentation, so provide it in hand-out form, and tell them you have done so, i.e. "I will cover the main processes briefly and for those of you that are interested in the details you will find full specifications in the hand-outs provided."

If you are selling an idea, *towards* people will be motivated to use it if it allows them to achieve something. *Away from* people will be more interested in what it will allow them to avoid. How will your idea help individuals who *sort by self*, and how will *sort by others* people be able to help others with your idea? Here's an example. "You will find this technology personally beneficial, and the service providers among you will be able to develop applications to help your client's business." By designing your content to cover the main filters (metaprograms, VKA senses, values and identity labels), you will connect on a personal level with more people and deepen rapport with more of your audience.

Recognizing these differences in people, and tailoring your presentation to include them all, will give each person in your audience the perception that you understand them, and that you are speaking directly to them. Assuming you have these points covered you can begin to sequence the material.

By designing your content to cover the main filters (metaprograms, VKA senses, values and identity labels), you will connect on a personal level with more people and deepen rapport with more of your audience.

■ Sequencing the material

There is a simple three stage structure you can use as an overall framework for your material.

1 Tell them what you are going to tell them (overview).
2 Tell them (give them the information).
3 Tell them what you have told them (summary).

People have a tendency to remember more from the beginning and end of a piece of information than from the middle. If you want to make it easy for people to remember your presentation, make the beginning and end long, and the middle short. Don't cram in too much information. There is a threshold of human tolerance for sitting attentively, and depending upon the entertainment factor this threshold is between 30 minutes and one hour. Forty minutes is an ideal period for a corporate-style presentation. Any longer than this and you may begin to lose your audience through the "numb-bum" effect.

When you have all your material, arrange it by chunk size first. Separate the large chunks from the small ones, and dispose of any that are not absolutely necessary for your audience to know. Your aim is to have the maximum impact with as few words as possible. The large chunks will be the main ideas, or headings, then smaller ones for sub-headings under each main topic, and finally the small chunks under each sub-heading. Be careful that a tertiary level is not too detailed or complex. Keep it simple.

An important point to remember when you are sequencing your information is to avoid making assumptions about what your audience already knows. If you recall, in chapter 2, I said that to make sense of new information a person has to link it to something that is already known. Think about existing knowledge as reference structures for new information, and avoid jumping too far from one topic to the next. Keep your words free of technical jargon, unless your intention is to really confuse your audience. Had I mentioned the term "metaprogram" in the introduction to this book, without explaining what it was, you might have been confused (unless you already knew the term). When a person is confused they are less receptive to new information because their attention is focussed on unraveling the confusion.

■ Humor

I always go for an informal presentation, even if my audience is made

Be careful that a tertiary level is not too detailed or complex. Keep it simple.

up of senior directors all in dark suits. Most people like to be entertained. Make them smile and you will connect with them. Spending an hour behind a lectern churning out monotonous detail with slide after slide and with nothing to break the pattern will cure the most acute insomnia.

Keep a list of jokes for different occasions. Make a note of amusing in-company anecdotes. You can get joke books on almost any subject, and you only need one or two to spice up your act. Often the best humor is directed at yourself – either as a quick one-liner or something spontaneous occurring during the presentation. Jokes and stories must have relevance to your subject, and should be delivered without an introduction. "Let me tell you a story . . ." "I have a joke about . . ." will warn people to prepare for humor, and you will set expectations for your audience which may not be met. Aim for a few smiles, not loud laughter.

Make them smile and you will connect with them.

■ Metaphor

As I arrived home from work one day last week, I came across my nine-year-old son talking with his friend Billy, who seemed to be having some sort of conversation with his dog. I asked Billy "do you always talk to your dog?" He replied "only when I'm teaching him to do tricks, and today I have taught him to whistle." "Well I don't hear him whistling" I replied. "I said I've *taught* him, he just hasn't *learned* to do it yet. Tomorrow he's going to *practice*."

If you really want to hammer home a major point, use a metaphor. The secret of a good metaphor is to keep it brief; use a different context; begin it without an introduction, and make sure the subject is relevant to the content and sequence of your presentation. Metaphors work at an unconscious level by conjuring up images in the mind and forming strong associations with the material.

If you really want to hammer home a major point, use a metaphor.

■ Notes

The fewer notes you make, the more natural and seamless your presentation will be. It is more useful for your notes to contain sequencing information rather than any material content which you should be totally familiar with. There are various formats for

Simple colorful pictures, concise clear dialog, and a sprinkling of humor will get you a result.

presentation notes. I prefer to draw a multi-colored mind map of the main topics which I only need glance at now and again, and I can see the contrast between the colors without having to get too close to it. Other people prefer cue cards (index cards are ideal), with one topic on each card.

Beware of using your projector slides as cues for your sequence. If your talk consists of speaking the same words your audience is reading on your slide, they will ignore one or the other, or both. Use visuals for pictures or bullet points. If you are showing a chart, keep the detail to a minimum – your audience will not thank you for giving them eye strain. Remember to work all the representation systems. Simple colorful pictures, concise clear dialog, and a sprinkling of humor will get you a result.

Language

The words you use, and the emphasis you put on certain words, are important. I think it is unnecessary to cover this in detail here as chapter 8 has covered all the angles you are likely to need. I will, however, point you in the right direction, and encourage you to think of how you can use Milton Model language to communicate to many people. Your mastery of artfully vague language will support you in many corporate level pitches, and keep you from getting bogged down with details that are either only of relevance to a minority, or something which you want to avoid.

And as your mind begins to process this information you can be assured that the author has only the best of intentions. We all have purpose in our lives, and whatever that purpose is for you, your mind is capable of creating the images that will make it a desirable and compeling purpose. And you may be aware of the process part of presenting, a part which can provide the key to your future as a presenter. A presenter people will enjoy listening to and watching, because you know just how your audience wants to hear and see information, and feel that you are talking to them – as the individual.

So far I have covered the areas you need to pay attention to when planning the content of a presentation. On the day things rarely go 100 percent to plan. It just isn't feasible to anticipate how your audience is going to interact with you, so you will need some process skills to deal with this, and as all processes are state dependent I will continue with your state.

All processes are state dependent.

State control

Top performers know all about state control. Feeling nervous is a natural reaction and the skill is to get your "butterflies" to fly in formation. Chapter 4 explained how it is important to design a "sixth strategy state" for any task that you want to accomplish with perceived ease and excellence. I will now take you briefly through what you need to consider in designing one for the role of presenter *par excellence*.

■ Identity

When you think of presenting how do you think of yourself? As a presenter, or a manager? When you are in front of an audience, do you want to manage them, or present to them? How you perceive your role will influence your results, so think of yourself as a presenter when you are working on your next presentation and notice how differently you approach the task of getting organized.

If you were to imagine yourself in your presenter role, giving a superb delivery to a large audience, what would you look and sound like? And what would it feel like to be totally at ease and in command of a large audience? Position your eyes "up to the right" and take a while to associate with this vision and intensify all the submodalities of the experience until you get the feeling of self-confidence – of being a professional presenter. And just before your state reaches its peak, anchor it to a unique stimulus. Now do this at least five more times using exactly the same anchor and you will have a resourceful state you can call up whenever you need it. It is worth backtracking over the material on submodalities and anchoring to help you create a high intensity state.

■ Values and beliefs

How important is it for you to be able to present to an audience effectively and professionally? What values do you have when it comes to presenting? Just suppose you are the professional presenter you can imagine yourself to be. What will that get for you, and what consequences will it have on other areas of your work and your life?

Your answers to these questions will expose your values and beliefs around presenting. Limiting beliefs like "I couldn't do that," or "I would look silly doing that," or "I don't have the right character or personality for this" will enforce an avoidance strategy. This is where your Meta Model precision questioning techniques will prove useful as you break down any limiting beliefs you may have. Answer this question: "what prevents you from doing it, now?" I'll leave the rest to you.

The important thing to remember is that you need to be aligned with your whole neurology. It's no use just doing a belief change, or working on identity. You need the whole thing. When you can "feel" a moving toward metaprogram driving you to become more capable at presenting you are probably as aligned as you will ever be.

Connecting with your audience

Getting and keeping rapport with your audience is vital in a presentation where you are expected to do the leading. In your opening lines, after you have introduced yourself and established your terms of reference, welcome everyone and give out comments that pace identity and values. For example:

> "I am pleased to have a mixed audience of business managers, support people and members of the accounting profession here today, and I extend a warm welcome to you all. I know that production of the Z200 analyzer is important to this area of the business, and you will probably have your own particular views on this. Whatever your interest in the Z200 my intention today is to . . . etc."

This opener paces identity and values in a non-specific way, avoiding assumptions about any one particular view or value.

■ Pre-framing

Put a frame around the entire presentation. This will prevent your audience from forming unrealistic expectations of you, and it will keep them focussed on where you want their attention. A pre-frame might go something like this:

> *"The information I will be presenting to you may raise many questions. However, the purpose of me being here today is to give you an insight into the new product development plant. I will be very happy, at the end of the presentation, to take questions which will clarify my information. Some of you may be curious to learn how the new plant will affect our European operations, and the marketing team will have an information pack available shortly on this."*

This pre-frame example sets the boundaries of expectation. It makes it OK for you to say "that detail will be included in the marketing information pack" during the question time at the end.

■ Physiology

Your state is affected by your physiology, so it will be important to sustain a posture that projects self-confidence and maintains your state. For most people an upright, relaxed, posture is best, with your head slightly up looking around the audience and establishing eye contact with individuals. Randomly select individuals and keep eye contact with them for about 3–4 seconds. This will give a clear message that you are really connecting.

Your state is affected by your physiology.

Breathing

The rhythm and depth of your breathing will influence your state tremendously. You want to come across to your audience as being relaxed, but not so relaxed that your delivery is slow and arduous. On the other hand you don't want to rush through your material at break-neck speed. Breathe deeply and evenly at a pace that feels relaxed to you. It's OK to stop talking and just take a couple of deep breaths to help maintain your state before you continue. If you

If you breathe evenly your words will come out evenly.

Keep your gestures clean and practice using them with precision.

breathe evenly your words will come out evenly. If you are a strong visual, slowing down your breathing may seem awkward to you at first. You can still breathe in the upper chest area while slightly increasing the length and depth of each breath. Kinesthetics who may breathe more slowly might want to experiment with a slightly faster rhythm. Whatever your natural breathing pattern, choose a rhythm that you feel comfortable with, and which helps to maintain a peak state.

Gesture

Practice talking and feeling comfortable with your arms by your side. Be aware of your fidgety habits and make a conscious effort to get rid of them. Hands in and out of pockets, twiddling thumbs, shuffling papers, rubbing hands and twirling pens are all fidgets. Keep your hands still and move them only when you have a clear purpose for doing so like changing a slide or making a gesture. We all use gestures of one kind or another, and they are mainly generated by the unconscious mind. Many of them are habitual. Be aware of your habitual gestures and build new ones into your presentations intentionally. Keep your gestures clean and practice using them with precision. Your audience will notice sloppy gestures.

Use your hands, arms, head and any other part of your body to make a point, or even anchor a state in your audience. If you have some humorous stories to tell, you can anchor a state of smiling in your audience by choosing a unique spot to stand on and making a unique gesture as you deliver the punch line. Stand in the same spot and give the same gesture with a unique voice tone and pitch each time you tell a punch line. Voice tone and pitch is a powerful anchoring stimulus.

Explore anchoring other states like curiosity, interest or agreement in your audience. Used well, and with precision, anchoring is a superb technique for generating intense states in your audience.

■ Voice

The voice has a range of tone, pitch, resonance, speed and volume. A good presenter will use the whole range of the voice for emphasis. Work the voice with the body posture and gestures to create rich messages for your audience. Make a point of listening to popular presenters and orators and noticing how they use their voice for different effects. Practice changing your voice to reflect the type of emphasis you want. From a deep, loud, voice to stress a serious point, change to a softer, quieter, voice drawing the audience's attention to a small, specific, but important, detail. Explore the range you have available and put together impactful combinations of voice and gesture for your next presentation.

Practice changing your voice to reflect the type of emphasis you want.

Handling questions from the audience

There are three basic requirements for answering all questions:

1 Never answer a question directly until you have determined the intention behind it. This is a distinction about *process*, not content.
2 Be in total uptime when you are asked a question so that your sensory acuity is high, noticing unconscious communication processes in physiology and voice qualities.
3 Keep emotionally detached. If someone has a question – fine. Deal with it. It is the information which is being questioned, not you. If you are asked a direct personal question it may be better to deal with it after the presentation.

Determining the intention behind the question is quite simple. Sometimes a questioner will provide it for you like this: "I have just started work in this area and would find it useful to understand more about this subject. What is . . . ?" Others will not be so obliging and will just ask the question "why does x mean that y is unsatisfactory?"

This "why" question may be straightforward, or not – to be safe ask the question "before I explain that for you it would help me to know your level of interest in this area." The answer to this question will reveal the intention behind the first question, and you will be able to answer more specifically for the questioner.

Some questioners enjoy getting feedback about the nature of their question. These will be the "externally referenced" people. You can make them feel OK by saying "that's a very pertinent question – thank you for asking it" or a variation around these words.

■ Hypothetical and judgmental questions

"What is your opinion about . . .?"
"What would happen if . . .?"
"How far do you think this can go?"

You can choose a range of responses to these questions, most of which consist of turning the question back to where it came, like a boomerang. For example:

"I'm not here to give my opinion but to present the facts. Do you have an opinion you would like to share with the audience?"

"That's an interesting idea. Let's see if we can work this out together. If x did y, what would you expect to happen?"

"I don't know the answer to that question. I wonder if anyone in the audience has an answer. Any takers?"

"What do you think?"

■ Questions or statements from confused minds

"What did you say the yellow band was for?"
"That doesn't fit with what you were saying earlier."
"How can this year's profit be higher than last year's when we all know that sales have taken a downturn?"

You probably want a "backtrack frame" for these types, and perhaps a "chunk-up" to a higher level. For example:

"Let's go back and cover that once more. I mentioned the idea . . ."
"I'll backtrack and put that into perspective with what I said earlier. The concept of the yellow band . . ."
"Let me explain that by first of all clarifying what I said previously. The overall income for last year . . ."

■ The personal attack

"How can middle managers be trusted with this?"
"What makes you think engineers will be capable?"

Personal attacks are simple to deal with. You need to direct criticism away from the person and toward the subject. Chunking up is also a useful technique, for example:

> "Trusting is something we all could do more of, and it will be important to trust the procedure designed by the production team."

> "This company owes its success to the capabilities of all its employees. They must be continually developed."

■ The direct challenge

> "What is the point of all this?"
> "I fail to see how this will change anything."
> "This has all been tried before – and it didn't work then."

These questions indicate that the person hasn't bought into your ideas because of a belief they are holding on to. You must decide one of two responses.

1 *Acknowledge the remark/question and move on*
   "I can understand why you have made that statement, however here is not the most appropriate place to deal with it. I will be happy to talk to you about this after the presentation."

2 *Shake the belief*
   "That's one perspective on this agenda. Tell me, what do you think the consequences would be of not making a change?"
   "What would get you to see it?"

■ Using your body

Your body is a very useful tool at times in dealing with people who seem to be on ego trips. These people often need to demonstrate to the audience and the presenter that they are experts in your subject. Always avoid getting drawn into a technical debate. Never get defensive. Stick to the process using the techniques explained in this section, and for added impact position yourself as closely as possible to the questioner. This will have the effect of putting him under the spotlight which is an uncomfortable place for most people. Using confident gestures at the same time will increase the impact even more.

The object of oratory alone is not truth, but persuasion.

LORD MACAULAY
(1800–59)
English historian

Dealing effectively with questions is a matter of process. The process consists of:

1 Acknowledging the question.
2 Identifying the intention behind the question.
3 Deciding whether to deal with it now or later.
4 Choosing an information frame within which to deal with the question.
   – Backtrack.
   – Relevancy challenge.
   – Evidence.
   – Outcome.
   – Ecology.
   – As-if.
5 Choosing a strategy:
   – Boomerang.
   – Chunking up.
   – Direct criticism away from person and toward the subject.
   – Shaking a belief.

The final piece of advice to help you deliver effective presentations is the most important. Practice. Just like learning to ride a bicycle, the first time feels a little awkward, and after a while it becomes a habit. Practice by yourself. Watch your physiology in the mirror, and record your voice to notice the characteristics. Rehearse your next presentation like an actor would rehearse for a play. After a while mass-influencing through the corporate presentation will become quite natural to you. Perhaps you want to choose just one or two techniques to practice for your next presentation. Take it one step at a time.

INNOVATION

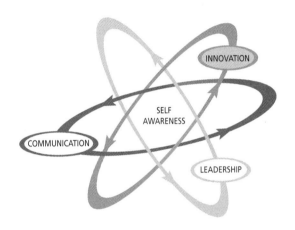

INNOVATION

SELF
AWARENESS

COMMUNICATION

LEADERSHIP

PERSONAL CREATIVITY

Imagination is not a talent of some men, but is the health of every man.

RALPH WALDO EMERSON (1803–82)
American Essayist
poet and philosopher

To create is to bring into existence, and to innovate is to bring in novelty.

"The best way to have a good idea is to have lots of ideas."

The two chapters in this section are dedicated to putting many of the techniques already covered in the book to use for stimulating the creation of new ideas. You may realize by now, having progressed through the material, that NLP is all about creativity and innovation – using different ways of thinking to create different results. The information in the book has been introduced to you in the context of managing yourself and your organization's resources. This section introduces you to combinations of the techniques that are particularly effective in creating innovative ideas for solving known organizational problems.

What is creativity and innovation?

To create is to bring into existence, and to innovate is to bring in novelty. So by these definitions it is possible to create many things which are not innovative. Creating a thousand ideas of a similar nature will not take your organization or your department into new realms of existence, whereas one innovation *can*, and the right innovation *will*. The Nobel prize winner Linus Pauling said "the best way to have a good idea is to have lots of ideas." So being creative is the pathway to being innovative.

There are few totally fresh ideas from which to innovate, however there are many existing ideas which can be taken from one context and adapted to fit another. For an example, consider the business franchise. The very first franchise was an innovation in the way a business could be grown and managed, but the idea had been in use for some time in another context, as a privilege of legal immunity or exemption. Before taking a look at the techniques, it is worth investing time identifying hindrances.

Hindrances to creativity and innovation

I am going to present four major hindrances which, in my experience, are the main constraints on creative thinking and on the generation of innovative ideas.

■ Habitual thinking processes

I have noticed that where the very nature of a job requires quick thinking, and where performance is measured in the time it takes to move from problem to solution, sometimes there is a tendency to move from problem to solution too quickly. This becomes severe when you begin to hear problems being described as solutions.

An example of this is where you might be restricted in your ability to increase production because the machinery is running at capacity. To say "we need to invest in more production machinery" is to define a solution, and in doing so blocks any other possible solutions from being created. It is more useful to say "we are producing to capacity with this machinery," and open up the potential for creating a wider choice of solutions, for example: contracting the extra work out, utilizing seasonal fluctuations in demand, reducing the amount of rework, etc.

Habitual thinking processes limit perspective (refer to figure 11.1). You can widen perspective on a problem by adopting different ways of thinking about it, and the techniques in this chapter are designed to do just that.

You can widen perspective on a problem by adopting different ways of thinking about it.

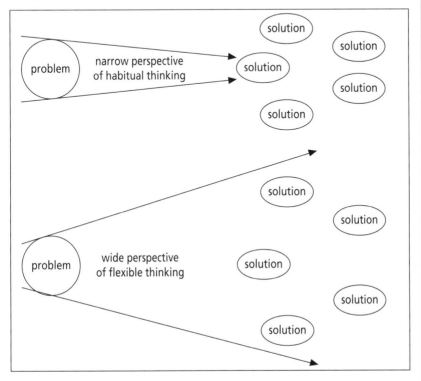

■ FIGURE 11.1
Perspective

■ In-time operators

Have you ever watched a group of eleven-year-old boys playing football? They become so totally involved in the action that they all follow the ball wherever it goes. There is no plan other than to get the ball, kick it in the general direction of the goal, and follow it. As they grow older they discover tactics and strategy.

Some people work this way. They are totally engrossed in what they are doing and spend little time in reflective thought. They are "in-time" (refer to chapter 2, figure 2.4), and their thinking style is action-biased. You can notice action thinkers when they are trying to learn a new computer software application. They would rather play with it than read the manual. They get through the working day by interacting with events almost entirely automatically with little reflective thought during each activity.

It can be great fun and very stimulating to remain "in-time," but you will need to switch between "in-time" and "through-time" to widen your perspective around a problem. Being "in-time" can have its advantages in problem solving. One of these is the tendency to generate "off-the-cuff" instantaneous remarks that are useful when brainstorming in groups.

■ Beliefs and values

Everyone has the ability to create and be innovative.

Contrary to what some people may believe, the marketing people don't have a monopoly on creativity and innovation. Neither do artists, poets, scientists or film directors. Everyone has the ability to create and be innovative, and the first place to begin making improvements is to examine your beliefs. If you believe you are not creative, or that your creativeness has limitations then that's exactly what you are likely to live up to.

A limiting belief can block you from developing your creative thinking styles – so change it to a belief that will support and encourage you to widen your perspectives on problems. It is also worth checking out your identity and values. If being creative isn't important to you, it is unlikely that you will put energy into developing your creative capability. Likewise, if you don't connect with innovation in some way as part of your identity, this will severely hinder creativity.

■ Language

Creativity and innovation require curiosity for which there is a language – the language of questions. There is another language in organizations – the language of action. During your next day at work notice what people say, and how often each language is used. The two languages can be related to the early metaphor in chapter 1, where the action language is used by people responding with *defeat*, *reaction*, and *sophistry*, while the language of questions is used by people responding with *curiosity*. Which language do people in your organization prefer?

The language of action consists of dialog that is about doing, achieving, analyzing, evaluating, utility, and necessity. The language of curiosity is less concrete, and more to do with contemplation, imagination, and possibility. There is a place and time for both these languages, but in some organizations action alone is rewarded, so people spend all their time doing and little time thinking and being curious. I will build on the importance of language by relating to thinking styles and different types of organizational problem.

Which language do people in your organization prefer?

Types of problems in organizations

I want to emphasize just two categories of problem – convergent and divergent.

■ Convergent problems

This category contains many of the day-to-day operational problems that may seem complicated and ambiguous on a first appraisal, but really all they need is a logical thought process to solve them. These problems are contained within a relatively small part of the overall organizational system, and they can be neatly funneled toward a specific solution. Convergent problems are easily proceduralized. It is possible to design a formula for solving future occurrences of convergent problems. Figure 11.2[1] represents a convergent problem. Notice your thinking style as you solve it.

[1] From Victor Serebriakoff, *The Mammoth Book of Puzzles*, Robinson Publishing; 1992.

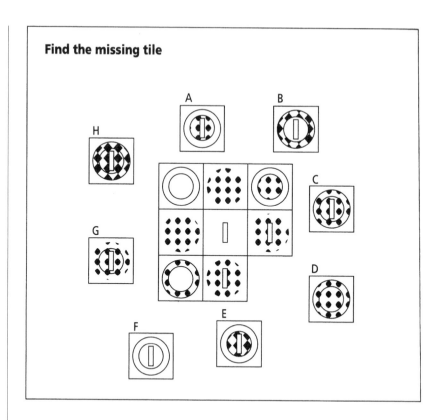

Find the missing tile

FIGURE 11.2
A convergent type
of problem

What thought process did you use to solve this problem? Many people begin by comparing the tiles. What you need to solve this problem is a formula or procedure based on relationships. The problem and solution are both contained within the information frame presented. The formula you need is: from left to right, starting top left X (first tile) + Y (second tile) = Z (third tile) and put the shaded circle to the back. The correct answer is tile C.

Can you imagine how difficult it would be to solve if each tile was part of a set of ten tiles with slightly varying designs, and there were nine other people all asking you for help to solve a similar problem? This is where the notion of divergence begins to take on meaning.

■ Divergent problems

Divergent problems tend to be influenced by a much larger part of the organization, and the more you attempt to apply a logical thought process the more divergent the problem becomes, often moving off into many different directions making it difficult to represent as one entity. Consider the following situation.

Resistance to change

Employees in the service division of a communications company seem to be uninterested in improving the quality of operational processes. They work hard and they get on well as a team but seem content to continue working with inadequate methods and procedures. They think that managers are responsible for fixing things, not them. The division has been struggling to maintain service levels and is now showing signs of resistance to the demand for improvements from management and from clients.

This is a typical convergent problem. There may be many reasons why people resist change, and once you begin to brainstorm these you soon fill up your flip chart pad. There could be any number of different dynamics acting all at the same time, and some of them may not be apparent on first appraisal of the problem.

A common response to these "people problems" is the sophistry response – investing huge resources into designing and implementing comprehensive quality measurement and improvement systems. Often the fundamental problem remains because the sophistry response provided a solution when what was needed was more curiosity to understand why the problem existed in the first place.

The small fry

This is an interesting one. An assembly plant manager wants to reduce the number of sub-standard parts which he receives from his company's various manufacturing divisions. His part of the operation is one of the smallest and contributes least to sales turnover for the group. Everyone seems to be busy on more important areas of the business. Even his own director spends most of his time looking after other responsibilities. How can the assembly manager convince other managers from manufacturing to involve themselves in an improvement plan?

This type of problem requires a strategic plan of influence and persuasion. The solution may not be contained within the information provided and so the problem needs to be opened up with a curiosity type of response.

Both these problems lend themselves more to a visual strategy over any other type of thinking. If you use internal dialog and the procedural style for these divergent problems you are likely to produce an inadequate solution. People are the backbone of organizations. It is possible to consider changes to processes without considering the influence of people, and to do this within the confines of an executive meeting room. However, to do so is extremely myopic and foolish. Listening, understanding, and involvement are the oil on the wheels of change. But to listen only with the ears over the telephone, is to disregard 55 percent of the overall communication (refer to chapter 7).

Managers who invest time in productive two-way communication with people will get more from their visual modality. They will notice more from physiology and voice tonalities. Many divergent problems are complicated because people are involved. If you remove people from the equation many organizational problems become convergent. Consider this simple scenario:

> *A manager decides that it would be a great PR exercise for all employees to wear badges saying "Total Quality Commitment." The manager gets everyone together and says "I want you all to wear these badges as a sign to our customers that we are committed to Quality." What actually happens is that the badges are worn – but only when the manager visits them.*

In this case, the manager in question didn't have the sensory acuity to pick up from non-verbal responses that there was an issue with wearing the badges. Not only that, but the issue isn't really about badges, it's about the way they are treated by managers generally. These signs will not register for people using the internal dialog, procedural thinking, strategy. It is more useful to be in a high state of "up-time" with a persistent curiosity mode of thought. This will increase your flexibility to deal with underlying divergent problems such as this one.

The wearing or non-wearing of badges may seem like an almost insignificant event, and in isolation it is. However, it brings to the surface the much deeper problem of unproductive manager/ employee relationships. If this issue were to be addressed it could have a much wider influence on significant areas like productivity, efficiency, effectiveness etc.

A strong visual strategy with auditory content and a state of curiosity will help to open up the space containing a divergent problem, but if you miss the 93 percent of non-verbal communication from people, you are also likely to delete this from your mental images. If you want to imagine how a manager, or a group might respond to a new procedure, you will get better quality information by generating high quality visuals containing physiology and auditory tonalities.

Visualization

Two of the most creative people this century were Albert Einstein[2] and Walt Disney.[3] They both had very well developed visual modalities, and they both spent a great deal of time daydreaming – engrossed in their inner movies. Einstein's early memory, which led to his Theory of Relativity, was of a daydream during a mathematics class where he visualized himself sitting on a beam of light. Einstein had the sensory acuity to notice that his thoughts were born from images. He developed his visual modality by suppressing words and thinking in pictures alone which removed boundaries to his imagination. Walt Disney used strong imagery to conjure up exciting new cartoon films, and he would also use sound and movement to create, in his mind, the full VKA experience for his audience.

Visualizing is better for divergent problems. Language constrains possibility. Yet, in many organizations, particularly those focussed on action and reaction, it is not acceptable practice to be seen staring out of the window. The ability to "think on your feet" is rewarded in action-oriented organizations, and I agree this is a necessary axiom for managers today. However, the quality of decisions made "on the hoof" will depend upon the ability to switch styles of thinking during a single conversation.

This next exercise is based upon Walt Disney's creative strategy

[2] Robert B Dilts *Strategies of Genius*, vol 2, Meta Publications; 1994.
[3] Robert B Dilts *Strategies of Genius*, vol 1, Meta Publications; 1994.

which will be explained in more detail in the next chapter. With practice, this exercise will help you to be more creative, innovative and decisive "on-your-feet."

 **EXERCISE 8**

Thinking on your feet

This strategy can be used in any situation requiring creative solutions to a problem being discussed. The context is not important.

1 Picture the situation and construct possible solutions (Vc). Let your imagination roam free – it's OK to be weird and unorthodox. Adopt the dreaming posture (head slightly up and cocked to left, eyes up right, breathe from high-chest area).

2 Criticize your visual idea using internal dialog (Ad). Adopt the critical evaluation posture (head slightly down, left hand on chin, index finger pointing up toward ear, eyes down left, breathe from mid-chest).

3 Imagine you have decided to go with a solution. What does it feel like to have accepted it? Feel for incongruency signals (Ki). Adopt the reality posture (head slightly down, eyes down right, breathe from stomach).

4 If in step 3, Ki = incongruent, repeat steps 1–4 using fresh visual ideas as the content.

5 If in step 3, Ki = congruent, repeat steps 1–3 with your solution as the content. If in step 3, Ki = congruent the second time around, trust your solution and go with it.

Close the pattern.

There is a variation to this pattern where you may want to choose between two ideas. What you do is to construct an image of each solution side by side at some point in the distance, and flit your eyes from one to the other looking for differences. Because this version is comparing two developed ideas, and isn't looking to create new alternatives, it is not necessary to look up right. The other steps are the same – take the solution which appears to be most appropriate and put it through the Ad and Ki processes. This is more of a decision-making strategy than a creative one, but it is extremely useful for making decisions "on the hoof." It is worth practicing this strategy, as it is possible to develop it so that the whole process can be completed within a few seconds.

Your natural state of creativity

Everyone has a unique state they put themselves into when they are being creative. Like everything else, your level of creativity will be state-dependent. A high intensity state of creativity will produce more and better ideas than a low intensity state. Therefore it makes sense to calibrate an intense state and anchor it for future access. This is particularly useful when you need to be creative for extended periods like brainstorming sessions and visualizing futures. I'll take you through the process.

You want to recall a specific time when you were being highly creative. If nothing comes to mind it's OK to imagine what it would be like to be highly creative. Now take this memory and visualize what you look like as you are being creative. See yourself being highly creative, and hear what you are saying and what others around you are saying. Now increase the critical submodalities – make the picture brighter, bigger, more colorful. Turn up the sound and pan it around. Now make the picture even bigger and three dimensional. Exaggerate movement and bring it toward you as you associate with it. And as you associate, be aware of your feelings inside and get ready to anchor this state in whatever way you prefer – just before it reaches its peak of intensity.

Repeat this exact same process, with exactly the same anchor four or five times, making sure that you "break state" between each one. The result will be an anchored high intensity state of creativity which you can access whenever you want to boost a future creative thinking process. The best time to anchor this state, or any state, is when you are experiencing it in the real world, so the next time you find yourself being highly creative, anchor the state.

Getting unblocked

Have you ever been in a state of such intense concentration and suddenly got blocked? It could be that you were writing an important letter and found yourself stuck for a particular word or phrase. It could be a convergent problem that required careful, logical, thought and your flow of thinking got locked into sameness. What actually happens in these instances is that the chemicals in your brain create neural connections that seem to form loops. What you need to do is break these connections to allow new and different connections to be made. When you are navigating your experience for ideas to use in other contexts – you are learning.

The process is the same. What you are doing is calling up an existing memory pattern and adding a new one to it. The brain, which has two halves – left and right – works through a complex and countless number of reference structures, or neural linkages. The left side of the brain processes information sequentially, one chunk at a time, and it controls the right side of the body. The right side processes whole pieces of information and controls the left side of the body.

This information will help to explain the seemingly absurd nature of the next exercise. It works by forcing you to use both sides of your brain simultaneously for speaking and moving the body to a unique pattern. It is guaranteed to unblock the severest of stuck thinking by scrambling the brain!

 **EXERCISE 9**

Scrambling the brain

A_L	B_R	C_L	D_T	E_L
F_R	G_R	H_T	I_L	J_T
K_R	L_L	M_L	N_T	O_T
P_L	Q_R	R_L	S_R	T_L
U_R	V_R	W_L	X_T	Y_L

Start at the top left and follow the alphabet through to "Y" and back again. Say each letter of the alphabet out loud at the same time as doing the following actions:

L = raise left arm and right foot
R = raise right arm and left foot
T = raise both arms and stand on tip-toe.

This exercise is best done standing up and vocalizing each letter. It can be modified for the office by using internal dialog and raising fingers and toes (it can be done discreetly at your desk without anyone noticing). Once you have used this pattern a few times it will start to become habitual. You can prevent this by mixing up the letters L, R and T to produce different patterns.

Enhancing creativity

How you enhance your own state of creativity will be unique to you. Whether you work at improving your visual, auditory or kinesthetic modalities will depend upon your current preference. Recent brain research has shown that creativity and learning can be enhanced by stimulating the brain in a number of different ways – emotionally, nutritionally, and physically/mentally.

■ Emotions

The brain learns best when it is emotionally charged, either negatively or positively. People easily recall emotional "highs" and "lows" in their life. Negative emotions create stress and so are not conducive to creativity. There is also a strong tendency to suppress negative or unpleasant emotions. It is better to create an environment where informality, humor and freedom of expression are acceptable.

Formal business environments stifle creativity. Music is a powerful way of accessing positive emotional states. Many of our positive emotional experiences will be anchored to particular songs or tunes. Some researchers argue that music with a rhythm similar to our pulse, such as Baroque, is best for learning. I prefer to think that any music which relaxes and helps to generate positive emotions will enhance creative thinking.

The eye of a master will do more work than both his hands.

BENJAMIN FRANKLIN
(1706–90)
American politician,
scientist and writer

[4] Eric Jensen, *The learning brain*, Turning Point Publishing 1994.

■ Nutrition

What you eat affects the performance of your brain. There is a great deal of information available today on healthy eating, not just for physical health but also for mental agility.[4] A high carbohydrate breakfast of bread and cereal is likely to reduce alertness. Fresh fruit, low-fat yoghurt, fish and nuts contain protein that is better for the brain. Protein contains the ingredients required to produce the brain's neurotransmitters for alertness and quick thinking. Reduce your carbohydrate intake for a few days and notice how it affects your thinking agility. Take a breakfast of fruit and yoghurt for a week or so and compare the difference.

Food combining diets are becoming more popular as a method of increasing overall energy levels through improved digestion and intake of vital nutrients. If you are going to invest time tuning (or re-programing) your neuro-linguistic capability it makes sense also to think about the biological well-being of your brain and your body. There are plenty of books available to help you choose a suitable diet.

■ Physical/mental

It is just as important to exercise the brain as it is to exercise your body. The two are components of the same system and influence each other, therefore it makes sense to invest time keeping them both fit. The brain thrives on variety and difference. Old people become senile when their brains stop being exercised. Many retirement institutions are considered as doors to the grave because of the routine existence which residents endure. Once the daily and weekly routines are learned, variety of experience is lost forever. It is the curious mind that is exercised more so than the reactive mind.

Sameness is habit forming. It is like putting a strait-jacket on the brain. Difference, change, and variety are brain stimulants.

This chapter has continued to build on the theme of thinking styles to increase behavioral flexibility. It has stressed the need to be more aware of how you think, and to explore a wider range of thinking styles to boost creativity and innovation. The next chapter will continue this theme for group creativity.

GROUP CREATIVITY

■ **A crucial question**

■ **Sources of problems**

■ **Techniques**

■ **Pictorial representations**

■ **Constructed representations**

The world we have made as a result of the level of thinking we have done thus far creates problems that we cannot solve at the same level at which we have created them . . . We shall require a substantially new manner of thinking if humankind is to survive.

ALBERT EINSTEIN
(1879–1955)
American physicist

The ability to choose your own creative thought process is something you have complete control over. This is not so with groups. Most will require at the minimum some form of facilitation or structural framework and training to help them break out of habitual problem/solution processes.

Quality circles and other such improvement initiatives are formal structures for helping people to be creative by applying a *curiosity* response to problems. Brainstorming is the most common form of group creativity process used in organizations today, and for many problems it is reasonably effective. Yet brainstorming is merely a high level process which can have many different variations using techniques to widen the problem space and increase both the quantity and quality of ideas. In this chapter I will introduce you to some different techniques to use in problem-solving sessions.

A crucial question

Among the many questions which will be asked during a problem-solving activity there is one crucial question – "what type of problem is this?" This question moves you to a higher level from where it is possible to get a clearer picture.

For example, a production line is having trouble matching its output to sales forecasts. Sometimes output exceeds requirement, and at other times it falls short. There are many arguments between production supervisors and sales about poor communication, inaccurate orders on the computer system and last minute changes to order specifications. As the company grows and sales orders get larger the problems become more severe and diverse with stress and frustration leading to decreased motivation and lower levels of productivity.

The words you use to define a problem will influence your solution. What type of problem is it? It could be classed as a problem of motivation, skill shortage, attitude, communication, process, timing or any number of other seemingly well-defined categories. Can you imagine the amount of solution resources that could be potentially wasted by committing an inappropriate solution to an ill-defined problem?

The words you use to define a problem will influence your solution.

For this particular problem scenario you need to go to a different level by asking more questions. You need to be at the level of process engineering – a systemic view of the sales and production functions – to notice the inability in each subsystem for achieving higher level organizational outcomes (meeting customers' delivery expectations). The process of questioning and diagnosis gets you to the right level of analysis, and it is often a different perspective of the problem that is the catalyst for locking thinking onto the right target.

Sources of problems

There are many different sources of problems, even when traced back to the highest common factor. I will first introduce you to 12 sources which I have found to be at the root cause of many organizational problems, and then go on to suggest ways in which you can use them in problem-solving sessions.

■ Perception

This exists where activity is driven by a perception of what is required rather than what is actually required. Are people delivering according to a perception of what their customers need because of poor communication links, or are product and delivery expectations discussed openly?

A manager inherited a large and politically difficult on-site computer service contract which, under previous management, had fallen to extremely low levels of customer satisfaction. People seemed to be working hard, but the client continued to emphasize concern at appalling performance levels. It took six months to turn the contract around to one of the division's highest performing contracts in terms of customer satisfaction and level of service.

I asked the manager what he had done to bring about the change. His reply was:

> *"It was a question of the perception held by the contract team. We had been taken on to manage the service, but the perception the team had was that they were there to be managed by the client and respond to their wishes."*

I then asked what he did to change that perception.

> *"I just explained the situation to the team. No-one had done this before. Once they understood that the client wanted them to take a management role they became more pro-active in reshaping the policies and procedures that were hindering performance improvement. We arranged client meetings with the purpose of discussing service management issues rather than defending a poor performance record which had become the norm."*

Perception-driven activity is a resource waster in any organization.

Team activity must be directed by actual customer expectations not perception. Perception-driven activity is a resource waster in any organization.

■ Relationship

Problems caused by ineffective relationships have many different dynamics. The symptoms of relationship problems manifest themselves in the breakdown of communication generally, and organizational environments provide a wide variety of causes. I have kept to three types of relationship causes which are sometimes the product of poor organizational relationship dynamics. You will undoubtedly be able to identify others in your own organization.

Mistrust

Trust is the foundation for productive communication.

Modern organizations utilize the power of the team. When teams are given the right direction and are pulling together they can deliver more than the sum of their parts. When teams are poorly directed they can close ranks and become competitive with other teams. This latter situation creates mistrust between teams. Trust is the foundation for productive communication. Where you have mistrust you have poor communication, and it is futile to attempt fixing anything else. Mistrust is a constraint on potential and a huge barrier to communication. People suppress ideas and information when they feel mistrusted. Can you recall a time when you communicated freely and openly with someone you mistrusted?

Territory

You have learned how people are different in the way they think and in their behavioral patterns, and you have only to observe the behavior towards each other of two people working side by side. One is a procedures person who values having an organized and tidy desk, while the other is an options person with a low interest in things and is generally untidy and less organized in the office environment. When behavioral profiles are opposites, situations can lead to basic environment and territory disputes. If you own the territory you can organize it to your own liking.

In large organizations people can feel that they own certain parts of the territory because they have worked there for a long time and put some of their personality into it. Territory can also refer to intellectual and process areas. I have noticed resentment and low co-operation from managers who consider they should have control of someone else's process or part of the organization.

Responsibility and authority

Where a transaction between two or more departments isn't producing the desired outcome it may be useful to examine the responsibilities and authority levels on each side. Responsibility must be continually realigned behind changing organizational needs and it is not useful to rely upon written responsibilities alone. There must always be a sense of responsibility which helps to form the attitude towards the job. Problems often occur when an individual, or a group, has a misaligned sense of what they are responsible for. "Sticking to the rule-book" behavior typifies this situation of which the "jobs-worth" disease is a classic example.

There must always be a sense of responsibility which helps to form the attitude toward the job.

Authority can be a block to improving relationship problems. Even where there is a good sense of responsibility a breakdown may occur because people are not given appropriate levels of authority. This is what empowerment is concerned with. *Authority needs to be balanced with responsibility.*

Relationship-type problems are often divergent, so even when you think you have put your finger on the root cause it is well worth staying with the problem and opening it up further. Attitude surveys, feedback questionnaires and communication workshops are all useful tools to help open up relationship-type problems.

■ Work design

The assembly line was pioneered and refined in 1912 by Henry Ford to produce the Model "T." This work flow design lasted for over half a century, and you can still find many examples of it around today. Ford, along with other large manufacturers, changed this basic design to incorporate technological inventions like the silicon chip and the robot. They also began to understand worker psychology leading to a team-operated production facility. The more recent drive for improved quality has led to an integration of the quality function into the workflow rather than as an appendage at the end of the product line.

As the pace of change continues to accelerate, the fundamental design of work flow needs continual appraisal. Business re-engineering is a methodology for achieving complete redesign of work systems. Problems are often related to outmoded, inadequate, or inappropriate work systems which can lead to relationship problems as each sub-system falls short of meeting its internal customer expectations.

The fundamental design of work flow needs continual appraisal.

Levels of learning, communication, and change

Enough has been said already in chapter 1 about how identity, values, beliefs, capability, behavior, and environment all influence results and are therefore all potential sources of problems. These levels can be used in group problem solving activities to open up problem space by applying different perspectives.

Techniques

EXERCISE 10

Multiple perspectives

Divergent problems require interventions in more than one area.

The more perspectives you can get on a problem the more information you will get as to the possible cause. Divergent problems require interventions in more than one area, and so there is always the danger that a solution to one perspective of the problem by itself will not be sufficient to effect the desired change. The "multiple perspectives" method of problem-solving can be adapted to include as many different perspectives as you think are necessary for a particular problem. I will explain the method using the problem types I have mentioned in this chapter.

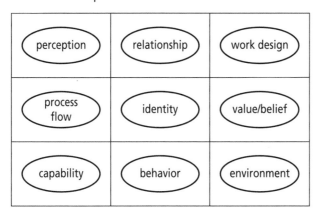

perception	relationship	work design
process flow	identity	value/belief
capability	behavior	environment

■ FIGURE 12.1
Multiple perspectives

With a large group of 20 or more

Each square represents a room containing a small group of between 3–6 people. Each room is labeled with a different perspective of the same problem. The groups brainstorm the same problem while remaining within the scope of their allocated perspective. The groups think of the problem "as-if" it were the type suggested by their allocated perspective. After a period of time each group presents the outcome of their brainstorming session to the whole team.

Most problem-solving sessions will perhaps include, at the very most, five or six different perspectives. However, if a problem is sufficiently diverse and a serious threat to the organization, all nine perspectives can be included by running the exercise over a number of days and taking, say, three perspectives per session.

With a smaller group

Vary this idea by allocating a different perspective to each member of the group around the same table. Another variation of this method is to use metaprogram perspectives (chapter 4) i.e. work patterns, activity content, motivational direction, level of activity, attention direction, reference sort, chunk size and group behavior.

Tips

Participants in this activity will require a thorough education in the whole process, and it will help to provide each group with a reference guide for use while brainstorming. The definitions of each perspective must be clearly put to avoid confusion between similar components like for example "work design" and "process flow," "behavior" and "capability."

■ The Walt Disney strategy

Walt Disney was perhaps one of the most creative thinkers of our time. His talent for creating animated films transformed the industry and built a hugely successful business empire. His high standards of quality, creativity, and perfection were an obsession. His films are a combination of exaggerated character features, stirring music, stories based on human morals, and vivid extremes of stillness and action to carry an audience through a range of emotional states. His most famous features included *Bambi* (1943), *Pinocchio* (1939), *Treasure Island* (1950) and *Snow White* (1938), all of which are still shown today on movie screens all over the world.

Robert Dilts, a long time developer of NLP, has studied the strategies of Walt Disney[1] and produced models for others to use. The underlying thinking style which Disney used to create new characters, stories and film settings was very specific. It consisted of three different phases of thinking:

- Dreamer;
- Realist;
- Critic.

[1] Robert B Dilts, Strategies of Genius.

The dreamer

The dreamer phase is locked into imagination, looking for possibilities of what could be. There are no constraints, limitations or evaluations connected to this mode. It is primarily a visual mode with a synthesis of sound and feeling. Disney would actually visualize symphonic music – giving it form – music being the lead to his preferred visual modality. The physiology associated with the dreamer phase is upright, with the head tilted slightly up and eyes up to the right (visual construct).

The dreamer phase is locked into imagination, looking for possibilities of what could be.

The realist

The realist phase is concerned with the "how" of implementation –

how the output from the dreamer can be put into action and made a reality. It does not seek to evaluate or criticize – rather to explore alternative ways of making the dreamer's vision happen. The key to being an effective realist is the ability to associate with different characters, taking different perspectives on the finer details of the dreamer's vision. In this respect it may be useful to adopt the physiology of each character.

The realist phase is concerned with the "how" of implementation.

The critic

The critic phase is one of logic and consequences. The critic looks for problems using a "what if" frame. To effectively criticize the work of the dreamer and realist, the critic must be sufficiently removed from the situation. The critic is concerned with getting it right. Everything must fall into place with no rough edges or unfinished actions.

This is not a negative stance, but a valuable contribution to checking out ideas and ensuring they meet established criteria. The critic can be just as creative as the dreamer by identifying a missing or inappropriate element of a plan. Critics should continually ask the question "what if?" The physiology of the critic is in critical evaluation pose with the head tilted slightly down and the hand to the side of the face or supporting the chin.

The critic phase is one of logic and consequences.

Using the strategy

It should be remembered that the dreamer does not have the monopoly on ideas. This is a creative process used to generate ideas and each phase is equal in its contribution to creativity. Without a realist and a critic the dreamer's ideas are unlikely to develop into actions. I will explain two ways of using the Walt Disney strategy in addition to the one in chapter 11 which was used for "thinking on your feet."

Disney's perceptual positions

EXERCISE 11

For small groups

This is based upon the same concept of space as used in chapter 3, only this time there are four physical locations labeled dreamer, realist, critic, and observer. The advantage of setting out physical locations for each perspective is that it helps to separate the different thinking patterns. I often find myself in meetings where problem, solution, and ideas seem to follow no logical process of thought or discussion. The typical result of this disorganized debate is confusion and inaction. The three Disney locations ensure that each phase of the creativity process is separated, and the observer location ensures that they are working in congruence with each other.

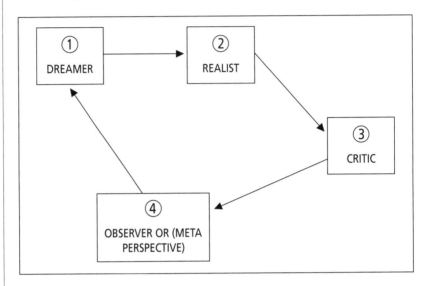

■ FIGURE 12.2
Disney's perceptual positions

Step 1
Write a brief description of the context and objective for which creativity is required. A visual image with the text will help to keep the group focussed on the objectives without having to break state to read. Pictures can be observed from peripheral vision.

Step 2
Organize the team into four groups. Ask each group to anchor a pure and intense state to each of the three locations – dreamer, realist, and critic. If the group are not skilled in anchoring you can help them to generate an optimum state for each location by inviting them to recall a time when they were a) dreaming, b) being a realist, c) criticizing.

Step 3
Associate with each location in turn, starting with the dreamer. Take as much time as necessary to ensure that states are pure before moving on to the next

location. In the dreamer location, use visualization sound and feelings only. Internal dialog is not a useful mode for creativity. In the realist location, take the images created by the dreamer and make them work. Associate with any characters that may be involved to get a realistic feel of how they will be affected by the ideas generated. From the critic location repeatedly ask the question "what if?" until all the possible problems and dangers have been overcome.

Step 4

Step onto the observer location and consider the whole creativity process happening between the three locations. Look for signs of incongruence and digression from the context and objectives.

Step 5

Continue to move through each position until there is satisfaction and congruence with the ideas generated.

A variation for large groups

As an alternative to moving through the perceptual positions, you can have each group remain with one perspective and pass the information around each group. You will need four syndicate rooms for this exercise. In room 1 will be the dreamers who are tasked with generating ideas and passing them to the realists in room 2. The critics in room 3 take the ideas from the realists and pass them to the observers in room 4. The observers do not alter the ideas, but give feedback to each group on how well they are keeping to the context and objectives. They should also recognize and feed back qualitative information about the content of each group's contribution.

■ The Einstein strategy

Most people know of Albert Einstein for his Theory of Relativity ($E=MC^2$). Arriving at this formula took Einstein many years. His very first thought on relativity occurred at the age of 16 as he was day-dreaming during a math lesson at school. He wondered what the world would look like if you were sitting on the end of a light beam. And if you were holding a mirror in your hand would you be able to see your reflection?

Einstein is regarded as a genius for his contribution to science.

[2] Robert B Dilts, *Strategies of Genius*, Volume II.

Robert Dilts' study of Einstein[2] gives an insight into his creative thinking strategies which can be learned and used by anyone. Here I want to present you with one example of how Einstein's thinking strategy can be used in a group creativity process.

The technique

Einstein preferred to think in pictures rather than words. Pure visual imagination doesn't have the associations, meanings, rules and structure that a spoken language has. If you think in words you are already influencing the quality and quantity of ideas which you can potentially generate. Only after thoughts have been generated is the spoken language of any use.

Some people may say that they don't see pictures, or that they don't visualize. What actually happens is that these people do visualize, but they have developed other representation systems in preference to the visual modality. Strength in the auditory system and internal dialog is very common among business people. The following is often a convincer for these people: *what I want you to do is imagine a green monkey playing basketball with a purple and yellow hippopotamus. Can you imagine that?* Of course they can. Now, it's time to visualize.

 **EXERCISE 12**

The instructions for this are simple. You first need a situation frame – some words that define the problem, and perhaps a system diagram showing the problem boundaries. Once the frame is set people are instructed to think only in visual images. They must tame their internal dialog – tell them that if it creeps in to turn it off and concentrate on the pictures.

Allow the imagination to take control of the thinking process. Relaxation music will help, and breathing high in the chest area will help to kick-in the visual modality. Suggest that they may want to lie down or close their eyes – whatever is the most comfortable. Allow the group up to 20 minutes for this process. When they have finished invite them to share their ideas with each other freely in small groups of 3–5. As each person explains their ideas, the other group members ask questions relating to perception, identity, values, and beliefs. For example, what identity would be most useful to carry out this idea? What values and beliefs would be needed to make this happen? What perceptions might people create around this idea?

The results can be documented for later evaluation. This technique can also be used for the dreamer stage of the Walt Disney strategy.

Pictorial representations

This technique utilizes the process of drawing pictures to delve into the unconscious mind for ideas. The concept of picture drawing is used by organizational consultants to help people interpret their perceptions of a problem. Here I will explain how you can use the same concept to open up problem space.

 **EXERCISE 13**

Explain the problem to the group and hold a 20 minute debate covering as many different perspectives as possible. This will expose much of the diversity around the problem. Supply plenty of A3 and/or A1 paper with lots of different colored pens. The objective is to allow the mind to think freely and imagine what might be causing the problem. As ideas begin to emerge they are represented pictorially. Explain that there are no constraints on what is drawn. Pictures may be of things, people, metaphors or abstract meaning.

What sometimes happens during this exercise is that as you concentrate on drawing an object, the qualities of the picture often challenge subjective views and opinions about the situation. Don't be surprised when people insist on drawing three or more different pictures because they have re-evaluated and changed their opinion or assumptions during the process. When everyone has completed their pictures pin them up on the wall and allow the group to observe each one, as if they were in an art gallery. Relaxation music will help people to reflect on the ideas portrayed by the images.

Follow this with an open debate around the ideas presented. This exercise can often expose different perceptions of the problem – and these perceptions are often part of the problem you are working on.

Constructed representations

This technique is similar to the pictorial representation except that the medium used is construction or modeling of some kind. It could be children's building bricks, a toy construction set, or some modeling clay. Try and offer a choice of materials to work with. Explain that the objective is not to demonstrate dexterity in building skills, but to construct, build, mould or sculpt a form which represents the problem being discussed.

 EXERCISE 14

I can never stand still. I must explore and experiment. I am never satisfied with my work. I resent the limitations of my own imagination.

WALT DISNEY
(1901–66)
American film cartoonist
and director

Follow the same process as the previous exercise, starting with a brief discussion to explore different perspectives, then a period of construction followed by a tour of the art gallery and ending with an open debate. Be prepared for the unexpected during this type of activity. It can bring out some deep-rooted perceptions, beliefs, grudges, moral issues and all kinds of things that were previously locked away in the unconscious mind.

The ideas presented throughout this section on innovation may be difficult for some organizations to accept with any notion of seriousness. That is to be expected, as organizations, like people, are at different stages of development with their own perceptual filters on the world around them. I have two cautionary pieces of advice for the adventurous.

1 *However you decide to change to become a more effective manager, make sure you pace your organization first.* I have noticed that if you take some people too far away from their comfort zone they rebel. This is one reason why we are all held back from achieving real potential. Pacing organizational values and beliefs is important if you are going to lead people to a better existence. Drastic and immediate change can confuse and alienate. Keep the rapport.

2 *Whatever you decide to do – believe in it in its entirety.* Have complete congruence in your purpose, intent and behavior. A half-hearted attempt supported by a shaky belief will not get you where you think you want to be. If there is an incongruence, don't act until you have sorted it out.

Epilogue

Injustice resulting from one person's assumptions about another person's behavior is sadly a common feature of organizational life. The frequency at which drastic personal consequences occur as a result of poor awareness, sensory acuity and general lack of understanding about people should be of great concern to business leaders. Talent can exist unrecognized in a jungle where status and power are valued over contribution and capability.

The change process from jungle culture to a learning and developing culture begins by narrowing the knowledge gap, among business managers, about the process of human communication. This process can be easily learned, practiced and used to improve not only the fortunes of commercial organizations, but the quality of life for employees and people in general.

Recently I was invited to witness a presentation by a group of young engineers who had been working on a solution to keep their workplace tidy. They formed a quality circle to work through the problems together. Initial attempts at introducing "tidy-up" policies were short-lived, but they persisted and generated some different ideas. After two months they had cracked it. Their solution was designed around three vital ingredients – education, involvement, and commitment. The solution itself may not be a mind-blowing feat, but the process which evolved to create it is whole-heartedly encouraging. This team will continue to solve problems because they have discovered a process of human communication which they enjoy. It is also productive, supported and encouraged by the manager, it gets desired results, and it improves the quality of their working conditions.

The young manager responsible for enabling this process has a great career ahead of him. He understands and is aware of the unique potential of individuals. His contribution to the business is not the result of a "quicker faster now" model of management, but on creating an environment where people can exercise their creative abilities and achieve more than just a quantitative result. Customer satisfaction is high, costs are reduced to a minimum and financial performance has been increasing for the past 12 months. This is the kind of thinking and behavior that organizations need to be modeling.

In the pages of this short book you have explored a discipline of mind and body technology – a discipline which is being practiced by more and more professional people in top organizations. People who recognize what it takes to be an effective manager in the information age – accepting the challenge of complexity and divergence – recognizing that, before anything else, the mind is an infinite resource which, after two million years of evolutionary existence on this planet, still remains largely untapped.

You will come across people from time to time who amaze you in some way – perhaps you might admire a highly developed skill for creative thought, problem solving, teaching, accounting, reading, developing teams, speaking or running an international business enterprise. These are skills which you can learn and master with perceived ease and excellence, and the first step is to *learn how to learn*. Once this is mastered there are few limitations on the skills available to you.

This book has been about learning to learn for managers. It has taken each component of your neurology, and with it explained the process of communication and programing so that you can begin to achieve more of the outcomes you desire. Remember – *to learn requires going beyond the edge of what you already know!* If that's an uncomfortable place to be, you have the knowledge of how to build a strong comfort factor into that experience – right now.

Here is a simple guide to help you practice NLP. It consists of three simple steps:

1 **Design outcomes that are well formed and ecological.**
2 **Use your sensory acuity to get feedback.**
3 **Be flexible to change according to the feedback you get.**

Enjoy the journey.

Glossary of NLP terms
(shortened)

Accessing cues Subtle behaviors that indicate which representational system a person is using. Typical types of accessing cues include eye movements, voice tone and tempo, body posture, gestures, and breathing patterns.

"As-if" frame Pretending that some event has happened. Thinking "as-if" it had occurred, encourages creative problem-solving by mentally going beyond apparent obstacles to desired solutions. Ask "What would it be like if I could . . .?"

Align Arrange so that all the elements being aligned are parallel, and therefore moving in the same direction.

Ambiguity The use of language which is vague, or ambiguous. Language which is ambiguous is also abstract (as opposed to specific).

Analog Having shades of meaning, as opposed to digital which has discrete (on/off) meaning. As in an analog watch (a watch with minute and hour hands).

Analog marking Using your voice tone, body language, gestures, etc. to mark out key word in a sentence or a special piece of your presentation.

Anchor Any stimulus that is associated with a specific response. Anchors happen naturally, and they can also be set up intentionally, for example, ringing a bell to get people's attention, or more subtle, standing in a particular place when answering questions.

Anchoring The process of associating an internal response with some external trigger (similar to classical conditioning) so that the response may be quickly, and sometimes covertly, re-accessed. Anchoring can be visual (as with specific hand gestures), auditory (by using specific words and voice tone), and kinesthetic (as when touching an arm or laying a hand on someone's shoulder). Criteria for anchoring:

- intensity or purity of experience;
- timing; at peak of experience;
- accuracy of replication of anchor.

Association As in a memory, looking through your own eyes, hearing what you heard, and feeling the feelings as if you were actually there. This is called the associated state.

Attitude A collection of values and beliefs around a certain subject. Our attitudes are choices we have made.

Auditory
Relating to hearing or the sense of hearing.

Backtrack To review or summarize, using another's key words and tonalities, or in presentations, a very precise summary using the same key words in the same voice tones as were originally used.

Behavior The specific physical actions and reactions through which we interact with people and the environment around us.

Behavioral flexibility The ability to vary one's own behavior in order to elicit, or secure, a response from another person. Behavioural flexibility can refer to the development of an entire range of responses to any given stimulus as opposed to having habitual, and therefore limiting, responses which would inhibit performance potential.

Beliefs Closely held generalizations about

    (1) cause,
    (2) meaning, and
    (3) boundaries in
        • the world around us,
        • our behavior,
        • our capabilities, and
        • our identity.

Beliefs function at a different level than concrete reality and serve to guide and interpret our perceptions of reality, often by connecting them to our criteria or value systems. Beliefs are notoriously difficult to change through typical rules of logic or rational thinking.

Calibration The process of learning to read another person's unconscious, non-verbal, responses in an ongoing interaction by pairing observable behavioral cues with a specific internal response.

Chunking Organizing or breaking down some experience into bigger or smaller pieces. Chunking up involves moving to a larger, more abstract, level of information. Chunking down involves moving to a more specific and concrete level of information. Chunking laterally involves finding other examples at the same level of information.

Congruence When all of a person's internal beliefs, strategies, and behaviors are fully in agreement and oriented toward securing a desired outcome. Words, voice and body language – give the same message.

Context The framework surrounding a particular event. This framework will often determine how a particular experience or event is interpreted.

Criteria The values or standards a person uses to make decisions and judgments about the world. A single criteria is composed of many elements, conscious and sub-conscious. The question to ask is: "What's important about . . .?"

Deep structure The sensory maps (both conscious and sub-conscious) that people use to organize and guide their behavior.

Deletion One of the three universals of human modeling; the process by which selected portions of the world are excluded from the representation created by the person modeling. Within language systems, deletion is a transformational process in which portions of the deep structure are removed and, therefore, do not appear in the surface structure representation.

Digital Having a discrete (on/off) meaning, as opposed to Analog which has shades of meaning.

Dissociation As in a memory, for example, looking at your body in the picture from the outside, so that you do not have the feelings you would have if you were actually there.

Distortion One of the three universals of human modeling; the process by which the relationships which hold among the parts of the model are represented differently from the relationships which they are supposed to represent.

Down-time Having all sensory input channels turned inward.

Ecology The study of the effects of individual actions on the larger system.

Elicitation The act of discovery and detection of certain internal processes.

Environment The external context in which our behavior takes place. Our environment is that which we perceive as being "outside" of us. It is not part of our behavior but is rather something we must react to.

Eye accessing cues Movements of the eyes in certain directions which indicate visual, auditory, or kinesthetic thinking.

Frame Set a context or way of perceiving something as in outcome frame, backtrack frame, etc.

Future pacing The process of mentally rehearsing oneself through some future situation in order to help ensure that the desired behavior will occur naturally and automatically.

Generalization One of the three universals of human modeling; the process by which a specific experience comes to represent the entire category of which it is a member.

Gustatory Relating to taste or the sense of taste.

Hierarchy An organization of things or ideas where the more important ideas are given a ranking based upon their importance.

Identity Our sense of who we are. Our sense of identity organizes our beliefs, capabilities, and behaviors into a single system.

Incongruence State of having reservations, not totally committed to an outcome, the internal conflict will be expressed in the person's behavior.

Intention The purpose or desired outcome of any behavior.

Internal representation Patterns of information we create and store in our minds in combinations of images, sounds, feelings, smells and tastes. The way we store and encode our memories.

Kinesthetic Relating to body sensations. In NLP the term kinesthetic is used to encompass all kinds of feelings including tactile, visceral, and emotional.

Leading Changing your own behaviors with enough rapport for the other person to follow.

Lead system The preferred representational system (visual, auditory, kinesthetic) that finds information to input into consciousness.

Logical levels An internal hierarchy in which each level is progressively more psychologically encompassing and impactful. In order of importance (from high to low) these levels include:
    (1) spiritual,
    (2) identity,
    (3) beliefs and values,
    (4) capabilities,
    (5) behavior, and
    (6) environment.

Map of reality (model of the world) Each person's unique representation of the world built from his or her individual perceptions and experiences.

Matching Adopting parts of another person's behavior for the purpose of enhancing rapport.

Meta Derived from Greek, meaning over or beyond.

Meta Model A model developed by John Grinder and Richard Bandler that identifies categories of language patterns that can be problematic or ambiguous. The Meta Model is based on transformational grammar and identifies common distortions, deletions and generalizations which obscure the deep structure/original meaning. The model has clarifying questions that will restore the original meaning of the message. The Meta Model reconnects language with experiences, and can be used for gathering information, clarifying meanings, identifying limitations, and opening up choices.

Meta program A level of mental programing that determines how we sort, orient to, and chunk our experiences. Our meta programs are more abstract than our specific strategies for thinking and define our general approach to a particular issue rather than the details of our thinking process.

Metaphor The process of thinking about one situation or phenomenon as something else, i.e., stories, parables, and analogies.

Milton Model The inverse of the Meta Model, using artfully vague language patterns to pace another person's experience and access unconscious resources. Based on the language used by Milton H. Erickson MD.

Mirroring Matching portions of another person's behavior.

Mismatching Adopting different patterns of behavior to another person, breaking rapport for the purpose of redirecting, interrupting, or terminating a meeting or conversation.

Model of the world A person's internal representation about the condition of the world.

Modeling The process of observing and mapping the successful behaviors of other people. This involves profiling behaviors/physiology, beliefs and values, internal states, and strategies

Non-verbal Without words. Usually referring to the analog portion of our behavior such as tone of voice or other external behavior.

Olfactory Relating to smell or the sense of smell.

Outcomes Goals or desired states that a person or organization aspires to achieve.

Pacing A method used by communicators to quickly establish rapport by matching certain aspects of their behavior to those of the person with whom they are communicating – a matching or mirroring of behavior.

Parts A metaphorical way of talking about independent programs and strategies or behavior. Programs or "parts" will often develop a persona that becomes one of their identifying features.

Perceptual filters The unique ideas, experiences, beliefs, and language that shape our model of the world.

Perceptual position A particular perspective or point of view. In NLP there are three basic positions one can take in perceiving a particular experience. First position involves experiencing something through our own eyes associated in a first person point of view. Second position involves experiencing something as if we were in another person's shoes. Third position involves standing back and perceiving the relationship between ourselves and others from a dissociated perspective.

Physiology To do with the physical part of a person.

Problem space Problem space is defined by both physical and non-physical elements which create or contribute to a problem. Solutions arise out of a "solution space" of resources and alternatives. A solution space needs to be broader than the problem space to produce an adequate solution.

Process and content Content is what is done, whereas process is about how it is done. What you say is content and how you say it is process.

Predicates Sensory-based words that indicate the use of one representational system.

Preferred system The representational system that an individual typically uses most to think consciously and organize his or her experience.

Presupposition A basic underlying assumption which is necessary for a representation to make sense. Within language systems, a sentence which must be true for some other sentence to make sense.

Rapport The establishment of trust, harmony, and co-operation in a relationship.

Reframing Changing the frame of reference around a statement to give it another meaning.

Relevancy challenge Asking how a specific statement or behavior is helping to achieve an agreed outcome.

Representational systems The five senses: seeing, hearing, touching (feeling), smelling, and tasting.

Reference structure The sum total of experiences in a person's life story. Also, the fullest representation from which other representations within some systems are derived; for example, the deep structure serves as the reference structure for the surface structure.

Resources Any means that can be brought to bear to achieve an outcome: physiology, states, thought, strategies, experiences, people, events, or possessions.

Resourceful state The total neurological and physiological experience when a person feels resourceful.

Sensory acuity The process of learning to make finer and more useful distinctions about the sense information we get from the world.

Sensory-based description Information that is directly observable and verifiable by the senses. It is the difference between "The lips are pulled taut, some parts of her teeth are showing and the edges of her mouth are higher than the main line of her mouth" and "She's happy" – which is an interpretation.

Second position Seeing the world from another person's point of view and so understanding their reality.

State The total ongoing mental and physical conditions from which a person is acting. The state we are in affects our capabilities and interpretation of experience.

Stimulus response An association between an experience and a subsequent so-called reaction; the natural learning process Ivan P. Pavlov demonstrated when he correlated the ringing of a bell to the secretion of saliva in dogs.

Strategy A set of explicit mental and behavioral steps used to achieve a specific outcome.

Sort A computer term meaning to reorganize and/or to filter information in the process of the reorganization.

Sub-modalities The special sensory qualities perceived by each of the senses. For example, visual sub-modalities include color, shape, movement, brightness, depth, etc; auditory sub-modalities include volume, pitch, tempo, etc; and kinesthetic sub-modalities include pressure, temperature, texture, location, etc.

Surface structure The words or language used to describe or stand for the actual primary sensory representations stored in the brain.

Swish pattern A generative NLP sub-modality process that programs your brain to go in a new direction. Is very effective in changing habits or unwanted behaviors into new constructive ways.

Systemic To do with systems, looking at relationships and consequences over time and space rather than linear cause and effect.

Third position When you observe yourself and others.

Timeline The way we store pictures, sounds, and feelings of our past, present, and future.

Tonal marking Using your voice to mark out certain words as being significant.

TOTE Developed by Miller, Galanter and Pribram, the term stands for the sequence Test-Operate-Test-Exit, which describes the basic feedback loop used to guide all behavior.

Trance An altered state with an inward focus of attention on a few stimuli.

Uptime State where the attention and senses are committed outwards.

Values Those things that are important to us and are driving our actions.

Visual Relating to sight or the sense of sight.

Visualization The process of seeing images in your mind.

Voice quality The second most important channel of communication and influence. Research suggests it is 38 percent of the total impact of the communication.

Well-formedness conditions The set of conditions something must satisfy in order to produce an effective and ecological outcome.

Further resources to help you manage with the power of NLP

Available from Quadrant 1 International – leaders in coaching, learning and change.

- Contact David through the website at: **www.quadrant1.com** where you will find a range of tips, tools and ideas to download from a growing database of practical resources.
- Subscribe to Aim for Success on the website and receive regular updates via email to help you *be* and *do* your best.
- Organise an NLP workshop for your team, group or company.
- Ask us about 1:1 coaching, and team coaching.
- Discover more about success in business through the following books:
  - *NLP Business Masterclass* by David Molden
  - *Realigning for Change* by David Molden and Jon Symes
  - *Beat Your Goals* by David Molden and Denise Parker.
- Discover how individuals, teams and corporations are putting these ideas to work by viewing the articles in the media section of the website.

How to contact the author

www.quadrant1.com
energise@quadrant1.com
+44 (0) 1865 715 895

index

245

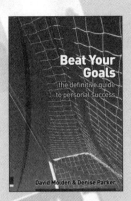